ENDORSEMENTS

For decades, Elinor Young has been a hero to me. Her faith has been forged by setbacks that would derail most of us mortals. For all who face adversity and seek joy and courage, this book is like flipping on a light.
    —Phil Callaway, best-selling author and host of *Laugh Again Radio*

In editing stories of disability in mission, I was struck by Elinor's. One clear reason is that Elinor recognizes the welcoming aspect of her disability among the tribal group in the highlands of Papua to whom she ministered and for whom she provided part of a translation of the New Testament. In true humility, Elinor allowed them to participate in her disability weakness by transporting her and assisting her in other ways. The photo of the people carrying her on a makeshift litter safely over a steep and dangerous cliff reminds us that our Lord lifts his servants high and safe, even if through the agency of others, to do his work in his ways. As a missionary in one of the world's most challenging settings, Elinor lived those incredible ways as she discovered that God uses people with disabilities, not in spite of disability but because of it.
    —Dave Deuel, PhD, coauthor/editor of *Disability in Mission: The Church's Greatest Treasure* Senior Research Fellow and Policy Advisor advocating for people with disabilities at the United Nations, Joni and Friends International Disability Center

What better testimony to support the thesis from our book *Disability in Mission*—that God has a way of using disability for his missional purpose. He uses vulnerability to show his surpassing love and power to those who don't yet know him. It's the biblical pattern. It's the pattern repeated in the stories in *Disability in Mission*. And it's the story of Elinor Young's journey.

I challenge anyone to read her beautiful account with a dry eye. You will be challenged to accept your own struggles and get on with serving God. He will turn weakness into strength. Shame into honor. Foolishness into wisdom. When Elinor Young, after polio, responded to a call to mission, others around her were embarrassed and felt sorry for her. The response of the dear missionary speaker was profound. "Whom the Lord calls, he will use." And did he ever use Elinor Young for his kingdom in reaching out to tribes in Papua!?

—Professor Nathan John, coauthor/editor *Disability in Mission: The Church's Greatest Treasure*

If you have ever wondered how God could use you in his mission, his work in this world, then Elinor Young's book will give you a much-needed perspective in answering that question. In multiple ways, the book underscores the truth that "Whom the Lord calls, he will use."

Running on Broken Legs is a vibrant reminder that it is not through overcoming our own weaknesses that we will become more useful to God in his mission in this world. Rather, it is by recognizing our weaknesses as an ongoing call to dependency on his grace and the work of his Spirit in us and through us. Ministry is ultimately "his business," as Elinor writes. As leader of the mission with which Elinor serves, I highly recommend that this book makes it into your must-reads for the coming months.

—David Riddell, International Director, World Team Global

Elinor has a great writing style, and she has a fascinating and inspiring story to tell. This is Elinor's story, but far more significantly, it is God's story—a story of God at work in a young girl in Washington and in a group of people around the world in Irian Jaya and how God brought them together to accomplish a profound work in each of them.

Her early experiences of hospitalization with polio developed her persistence and independence and deepened her trust in God—all of which significantly prepared her for missionary service in a difficult and remote area.

God knew where he could fruitfully use her adventuresome spirit, love for people, curiosity, enjoyment of languages, and willingness to try new things, along with her ability to cheerfully work around her physical limitations.

Was it worth it? Worth it for the Kimyal—from a handful of believers when she and the team arrived, to eighteen years later many believers able to read the Bible in their own language, and multiple church congregations led by local pastors and even sending out their own missionaries. And worth it for Elinor. "Korupun is in my bones and in my soul. It is where God showed me that he is enough. More than enough."

—Betty Sue Brewster, coauthor of *Language Acquisition Made Practical*
and founder of numerous international language acquisition courses

As the author of a book for children about the work of God in Papua, Indonesia (which included a chapter about Elinor), I found Elinor Young to be a true modern-day hero who lived the kind of nothing-is-impossible-with-Christ life that all children and young people can aspire to. I'm so very glad to know that she has written her memoir, and I know that those who read it will be deeply blessed.

—Rebecca Davis, author of the Hidden Heroes series of children's books

As a child, Elinor would play with her cousin, my wife, Michele, at Elinor's family farm in Chattaroy, Washington. Michele said that Elinor was always a happy child even though she suffered severely from polio. Incredibly, she spent time in an iron lung as a child, to as an adult living in the remote Korupun Valley in Papua, Indonesia, with her "bad legs."

I first met Elinor when I asked her to give a presentation to our local Shriners Club. From that day forward, I was one of her biggest fans. She gave a powerful and moving speech that night to our Shriner family. When she asked me to endorse her book, I was ecstatic!

Reading her book was a tearful, joyful, and thrilling ride. This book should be given as a gift to everyone you know. A very easy way to witness how God works.

—James Stewart, Chairman of the Board Emeritus,
Shriners Hospital for Children-Spokane.

What an amazing story of accomplishment and adventure! A disabled woman who overcomes insurmountable odds to be a missionary and Bible translator in the remote and inhospitable mountains of Irian Jaya, Indonesia. Elinor had to rely on God's strength because she had little of her own.

I met Elinor in 1991 at a post-polio support group meeting. We were discussing how we, as a group of forty-year-olds, were dealing with a sudden and significant loss of physical ability and the severe depression that went with it. Elinor, when it was her turn to speak, said that although she was feeling grief over the loss of her life's work, she had peace and joy because of her relationship with Jesus Christ. I was stunned. I had never heard anything like this before. That was the beginning of a long-term friendship. Elinor taught me how to have that peace and joy in my life. Her message of God's love gave me hope and literally saved my life.

—Sharman Collins, founder and leader of the former
Polio Experience Network of Spokane, Washington

RUNNING
ON BROKEN
LEGS

My Journey to Joy

RUNNING
ON BROKEN
LEGS

Elinor Young

REDEMPTION PRESS

Published by Redemption Press, PO Box 427, Enumclaw, WA 98022.
Toll-Free (844) 2REDEEM (273-3336)

Redemption Press is honored to present this title in partnership with the author. The views expressed or implied in this work are those of the author. Redemption Press provides our imprint seal representing design excellence, creative content, and high-quality production.

The author has tried to recreate events, locales, and conversations from memories of them. In order to maintain their anonymity, in some instances the names of individuals, some identifying characteristics, and some details may have been changed, such as physical properties, occupations, and places of residence.

ISBN 13: 978-1-64645-574-4 (Paperback)
978-1-64645-573-7 (ePub)
978-1-64645-572-0 (Mobi)

Library of Congress Catalog Card Number: 2021922445

DEDICATION

My parents were the best. With my whole heart I thank them for trusting that God knew what he was doing with me.

FOREWORD

Several years ago, I saw a video online that had gone viral. It began with an airplane approaching a short runway on the side of a mountain somewhere in Papua, Indonesia. After the plane safely landed, an excited crowd pressed around it. From the cargo bay emerged the very first copies of the recently completed Kimyal New Testament. The people were ecstatic, entirely beside themselves with joy. They danced and wept over the fact that after thousands of years, their tribe finally had God's Word in their own tongue. I remember vividly how the video made me cry. It turns out that one of the driving forces behind that translation was Elinor Young, the author of the book you now hold in your hands.

"Whom the Lord calls, he will use" are words you will encounter early in this story—words uttered by an unlikely character. As Elinor's life unfolds on these pages, this statement proves astonishingly accurate. I was utterly captivated, beginning with the wrenching account of her illness as a little girl, the iron lung, and her struggle to simply breathe. Along with her church congregation, I felt the awkwardness as she hobbled forward on crutches to commit her life to missions. I found myself cheering for her, agonizing with her, and then laughing alongside her as this incredible journey progressed. Exquisite attention to detail will make you feel like you are standing next to Elinor on the misty mountain highlands of Papua, Indonesia, living an incredible adventure.

While her skilled pen makes for an easy and enjoyable read, at the very core of this book are the numerous raw accounts of humanity encountering the Divine. Stories of God using the unexpected to bring joy and new life. *Running on Broken Legs* will encourage, challenge, and inspire you to attempt great things for the King, no matter what your circumstance.

Ian Bultman
Creator of Brinkman Adventures audio dramas

CONTENTS

PART I: POLIO: I LEARN TO COPE

Chapter 1—Change 17

Chapter 2—Polio 19

Chapter 3—New Identity 23

Chapter 4—Hospital Life 29

Chapter 5—Home Again 33

Chapter 6—Reentry 35

Chapter 7—The "Body Shop" 39

Chapter 8—My Expanding World 45

Chapter 9—Which Path? 49

Chapter 10—My Choice 53

PART II: I PREPARE TO FOLLOW MY DREAM

Chapter 11—To the Snowy North 57

Chapter 12—Lots to Learn 59

Chapter 13—Tools for My Skill Bucket 63

Chapter 14—Bigger Challenges 67

Chapter 15—Practical Preparation 69

Chapter 16—More School 73

Chapter 17—"In" or "Out"? 79

Chapter 18—Solo Cross-Continent Drive 83

Chapter 19—Building My Team 85

Chapter 20—Not the Nanny 89

PART III: IN A NEW WORLD

Chapter 21—First Introduction to Indonesia 93
Chapter 22—Irian Jaya at Last 97
Chapter 23—Cultural Impressions 103
Chapter 24—What's Ahead? 107
Chapter 25—Another World 109
Chapter 26—Adjustments 115
Chapter 27—Which Tribe? 121
Chapter 28—A Delay in Plans 125
Chapter 29—Troubling News 131
Chapter 30—A Trip to Soba 133
Chapter 31—Kamur: Visit to the Lowlands 139

PART IV: LIFE AND WORK AT KORUPUN

Chapter 32—First Visit to Korupun 145
Chapter 33—I Begin Life at Korupun 149
Chapter 34—More Firsts 153
Chapter 35—A House of My Own 157
Chapter 36—Prayer, Violence, and Demonism 161
Chapter 37—Grief, Comfort, and Goals 167
Chapter 38—Shaken 171
Chapter 39—Juggling Roles 179
Chapter 40—Mountain Climbing 185
Chapter 41—Amateur Tropical Medicine 189
Chapter 42—The End of the Beginning 195
Chapter 43—New Teammates, New Progress 199
Chapter 44—Mom's Visit 203
Chapter 45—Siud, a Changemaker 207
Chapter 46—Nurse Elinor 213
Chapter 47—A People Transformed 215
Chapter 48—A Growing Church 221
Chapter 49—Battles with Disease and Depression 225

PART V: MY TRANSLATION WORK EXPANDS
AND THE KIMYAL CHURCH GROWS

Chapter 50—Translating Bible Books and Stories 229

Chapter 51—A Hydro Plant for Korupun 233

Chapter 52—Translation Stories 239

Chapter 53—Kimyal Missionaries 243

PART VI: MY BODY REBELS

Chapter 54—Bad Legs 247

Chapter 55—Unhappy Legs, Angry Ticker 249

Chapter 56—What to Do? 253

Chapter 57—I Leave Korupun 257

PART VII: I SAY GOODBYE AND FIND PEACE

Chapter 58—Goodbye to My Kimyal Friends 259

Epilogue 261

Acknowledgments 263

Chapter 1

CHANGE

It is 1991. Nineteen years ago, the Kimyal people of the Korupun Valley in Irian Jaya, (the province now called Papua), Indonesia, butchered their last human victim on the rock where I sit. Now I chat with my Kimyal friends in their language, fluently and without fear. A few men wear shorts. Most of them wear traditional gourd penis sheaths. The women wear grass skirts and nothing else. Long ago all that became normal to me.

I smile.

"Ee sum nene na besarob log-ee" (Today's weather is wonderful), I say, then think, *Almost eighteen years here, with all the highs and lows. From angry bow-and-arrow fights to joyful baptisms, from happy births to dreadful murders. I love these people and their mountains. I can't imagine the day when I will have to leave them and this lifestyle behind.*

Here in the heart of Irian Jaya, in the eastern highlands, the mountains of my friends' beautiful world rise high and tight around us in all directions. I hear the power of the river near us as it crashes by, dropping 1,000 feet in its mile run through the valley. Waterfalls dash down the cliffs around us.

We are at one-mile elevation and just six degrees south of the equator. Today's rare and brief sunshine feels warm and welcome even though the air is cool. The light wind's scents carry evidence of all it passes over: bare rocks, tall clay-rich garden mounds and the sweet potato vines that cascade down them, trees high on the mountains and the orchids that live in their shelter, the strong reed-like grass on the roofs of the Kimyal's small, round huts in the scattered

17

villages, and the cooking-fire smoke that filters through those grass roofs. It all blends into freshness, purity.

Just as the wind-carried odors merge to produce something clean, the intermingling of the terrible and delightful times here merge into joy and contentment.

How much I have learned about the Kimyals, about myself, about the marvelous flora, fauna, and geology of this place, and about God.

I feel change coming into my world. New weakness and pain inhabit my legs. Polio-affected legs. I try to hush another voice emerging. It says, "You recognize this. You have been here before."

Chapter 2

POLIO

"No! You can't do this to our little girl!"

Mom and Dad's cry was to God, not to the doctors. I was in the hospital with polio, and I was just five years old.

It was January 1, 1952. The nation was seized by fear, in the grip of a huge polio epidemic. Everyone knew someone hit by polio, and they were terrified. During previous summers, swimming pools and other places thought to harbor and spread polio were shut down. Authorities quarantined homes of polio patients. Polio was the most feared national enemy. The January 1, 1953, *Spokesman-Review* newspaper described 1952 as "the worst year yet" for polio where I lived in Spokane County, Washington State.

When I woke that morning, I had never before felt such hot pain at the base of my head and lower back. I heard the usual breakfast noises in the kitchen below my bedroom. My sister and my three brothers were already up and in the kitchen. Milk buckets clanged as Mom washed them, and a kettle whistled on the wood-burning cookstove. It was cold upstairs but would be toasty warm in the kitchen. I got out of bed and walked to the top of the stairs.

Why are my legs so weak? I stood at the top of the stairwell. There were no handrails, and I knew I couldn't make it down. I called out, but no one could hear me through the door at the bottom of the steps. Trying to hug the wall, I carefully lowered myself down each step. With four steps to go, my legs collapsed. I tumbled the rest of the way, hitting the stairway door and causing it to rattle. My parents recognized that rattle, ran to open the door, saw me sprawled there, picked me up, and laid me on the living room couch. I couldn't move.

Dad ran to the phone and put it to his ear. Thankfully, no one was on our four-party line. Dad dialed our family doctor, Dr. Brown.

"Drive her into Spokane, to my office, and I'll meet you there."

While Dad ran to make sure the cows and chickens had food and shelter, Mom directed thirteen-year-old Margaret on the care and feeding of my other siblings: ten-year-old Ernie, three-year-old Harlow, and eighteen-month-old Dick. Mom put me in a coat, and Dad wrapped me in a blanket as well. It was January first and icy cold.

My parents had heard the radio's public service announcements that warned about polio and described its symptoms.

"No! It couldn't be that. Please no."

I don't remember anything about that drive, but I do remember the office visit with Dr. Brown. He put something in front of my face so I couldn't see what he was doing, then he poked and scratched me with a pin in various places.

"Do you feel that?" I didn't flinch, not only because I couldn't move but also because I couldn't feel the prick. All I knew was the loud pain at the back of my head and lower back.

Dr. Brown told my parents, "It isn't meningitis. It's polio. Take her to St. Luke's hospital. I'll meet you there." St. Luke's was the polio hospital for eastern Washington State. Patients, mostly children, were so many that staff emptied supply rooms to hold beds. They converted visitors' waiting rooms and the windowed play-room into patient rooms. Beds even lined the hallways, waiting for spots in rooms.

When we reached the hospital, snow fell as Dad almost trotted, carrying me down the sidewalk to the emergency entrance. I was still inside the blanket.

"Hurry, Daddy. I can't breathe."

I may have gone unconscious. Encephalitis, inflammation of the brain stem and membrane around the brain, is part of polio.

The next thing I remember is waking up in a white world. White curtains surrounded my bed, and white sheets covered it. All white like the snow outside. I still couldn't move, and I struggled to breathe.

Where are Mom and Dad? What is wrong?

I did not know, of course, the desperate prognosis. Both bulbar and spinal polioviruses were active in my body. I could die, doctors said, and if I lived I would most likely be an invalid.

Many years later, when I was well into adulthood, Mom told me about my parents' cries to God during those early days while the polioviruses were attacking my central nervous system. Bulbar (brain stem) polio attacks automatic functions like breathing, heartbeat, swallowing, and more. Spinal polio attacks the motor neurons up and down the spinal column. These go to the voluntary muscles of the arms, legs, and trunk.

My parents' initial demand to God was, "No! You can't do this to our daughter." As my condition continued to worsen, the plea became, "Please, please help our little girl survive." I grew still worse until my parents said to God, "She is yours. You may do with her as you wish." At that point, my physical state turned around. I would at least live.

Chapter 3

NEW IDENTITY

No one knew how far I would recover muscle strength, if I did.

Polio viruses destroy or weaken motor neurons attached to muscle fibers. Like cutting a landline telephone wire, a destroyed or damaged motor neuron no longer sends a signal to its assigned muscle fibers. The muscle doesn't get the message to contract, so it doesn't. If the virus just injures but does not kill a motor neuron, the neuron may sprout extra axon fingers and attach them to orphaned muscle fibers—those whose original neurons are dead. That process can take a long, long time, especially when all motor neurons are in some way affected, as they were in my body. These new sprouts aren't as robust as the first neurons, but at least the brain can talk again to the muscle fibers that have even weak neurons. Only a few live sprouts meant a weak muscle but are a reason to celebrate that there is some movement.

As I lay in my bed unable to move, doctors could only hope that a good number of new neurons would eventually sprout in my body.

Shortly after I regained consciousness, the curtains parted, and Mom and Dad were there, their faces behind white masks. It helped to know they knew that I was there, and I knew that they would be back.

In 1952, hospital visitors, including parents, were as unwelcome as tourists on battleships. Staff considered all visitors to be interruptions to the smooth routine, so they limited visiting days and hours. Most of the time I was alone, unable to move. I heard unknown sounds outside my curtains but saw another person only when a nurse or doctor came into my space to tend to something.

The memories I have of those first days are vivid but are just snatches, carrying no chronology, like old movie cuttings left on the editor's office floor.

In one scene, I lie on my bed and feel death creep from my feet up my body. I know I am dying. No one is around, but I know God is. "Please help me," I say to him in my mind. Suddenly everything is right. I know God fixed it.

In another scene, I struggle to breathe and suddenly see a doctor over me. He says, "Hold on, honey, it'll be OK in a minute."

That must have been when they put me in an iron lung. This was a tubular negative pressure respirator. The patient lay on a pallet inside the tube. Her head was outside the tube, and a seal was around her neck. Air pumped out of and back into the tube created the alternate change in pressure that caused the person's lungs to expand and contract. In that way, the machine breathed for them.

Afraid that I would become too dependent on the iron lung, the doctors took me out as soon as I could breathe, even shallowly, by myself. Mom told me years later that during that time I was able to say just One. Word. Per. Breath.

My improvement was gradual, of course. I'm not sure how long I was in isolation (now called ICU), but it was long enough for two formative impressions to settle on my consciousness. One was that God was with me and cared for me. The other I can best explain by the story that formed it.

I was lying in my bed unable to move, surrounded by curtains that kept me from seeing anything in the room. In that era, TVs were not common anywhere, and there was no entertainment in a child's hospital room or cubicle. A happy environment wasn't in anyone's mind. The medical community did not yet see that mental well-being is vital to physical recovery.

In those days, rules did not allow siblings under age fourteen to visit. Parents or other visitors could see a child for only brief periods on prescribed days. Doctors informed but did not consult parents about their child's condition and treatment. Neither parents nor doctors questioned this status quo. Those were the policies, beliefs, and ways of that time. Doctors and their rules were mini-gods, and that was the way it was.

This hindsight understanding does not diminish the effect of those ways though. For a child who was one of five siblings, the long days of fighting to live, punctuated only by occasional treatment visits by medical staff, were distressingly dreary. One day I was particularly bored. When a nurse came to check on me, I asked him if he could read me a story.

"Do you think you are the only child here? I don't have time for that." His face mirrored the impatience of his words.

The fact is, I didn't know there were other children outside my curtains—lots of them. How could I? Besides, I was just five years old. I needed human presence and was used to love. That day I understood that when not at home, I had to be "good" to be treated well. Good as in "not a bother" to anyone.

As I write this, I cry for that five-year-old the tears she didn't dare cry then. My instinct knew that I had to save all my strength and energy for the fight to recover.

When the viruses were no longer active in my body, hospital staff moved me out of isolation into a regular room. My sister Margaret turned fourteen on the last day of March, so she could visit me when my parents did. A take-charge kind of person, Marg was not a bit shy about using this privilege as she confidently walked through the halls to my room. I could only see Ernie, Harlow, and Dick through a window.

I wish I could talk to them.

At least I could look outside now. From my window, I could see children next door in the playground of the Shriners Hospital for Crippled Children, now Shriners Hospital for Children.

I wish I was there. It looks like a lot more fun than here.

My improvement was gradual. It was three months after I entered the hospital before I could move anything. New motor neuron axon sprout growth usually shows up first in the extremities. It took three months for enough axons to reach my toe muscles so they could hear the command, "Move!" They were the first muscles to get the message. I remember well the day they did.

A doctor stood over my bed, pulled back my sheet, and asked me to wiggle a big toe. I concentrated hard, trying to do as he asked. My right toe wouldn't respond, but my left one did. I could wiggle it! Only that one toe, but the doctor's response would make you think I had won a race. His face lit up, and he said, "That's it. You did it!" After that day I gradually gained the ability to wiggle all my toes, then my feet and my fingers.

Another memory stands out. One evening following lights-out, I felt thirsty. There was a glass of ice water on the bedside stand, but I couldn't lift it. I didn't even have enough strength to reach for it. But by then I had gained enough strength in my fingers to use them like crabs' legs to crawl my hands to what I wanted to reach. So I did my crab-like finger crawl to get my hand to the glass of water and managed to fish out a piece of ice. I brought it to my mouth by holding it the best I could with a few fingers and crawling my hand with others. I got the ice chip to my mouth but not in it. The ice chip slipped out of my hand and lodged under the back of my neck. Boy, was that cold! I didn't want to call a nurse for such an embarrassing thing, and I couldn't move or turn over, so I just lay there until the ice melted. By morning, the puddle had gone.

As I gained more use of my hands, nurses taped rolled pieces of rubber into cylinders that I could squeeze to strengthen my hands and to keep my thumbs in a correct position. When I could move more muscles, I began regular physical therapy.

Mr. Carper, the physical therapist, was a kind man who cajoled me into doing what I didn't think I could do. Or didn't want to do. Therapy sessions were often long, tiring, and sometimes painful. Atrophied muscles complained at having to move again. My brain got tired of telling them to work. Mr. Carper would pick up a leg, bend it at the knee while he placed his hand on the sole of my foot, and tell me to push. "Push! Think 'push!'" he would say, trying to retrain my brain to send the command and for my muscles to respond to the order.

Some days the brain and muscle work was exhausting. I remember being on the exercise mat one day and refusing to roll over one more time. I had had enough.

Many years later, in a post-polio support group meeting, the then-retired Mr. Carper told a story I didn't remember:

"Elinor was crawling on the exercise mat," he said, "and I told her, 'You look like a snake, crawling like that.'

'I do not!' she countered.

'Yes, you do.'

'No, I don't! Snakes don't crawl with arms and legs.'

'How do they crawl then?'

"After some thought, Elinor replied, 'They crawl with their all-together. Except their eyes.'"

Hearing that story made me smile because it and my own memories of those hospital days show me a little girl who had a confident self-identity. An identity that stayed intact while growing up visibly different from children who could run, jump, ride a bike, walk without a "galumph," bat a baseball, and carry their books to school.

As I meet other polio survivors, I see that not all of us came through this devastating disease with such confidence—and no wonder. Some endured unmerciful teasing at school or were shunned by people who didn't know how to react to someone who is nonstandard. My power to refuse to internalize society's insults, rebuffs, and misdescriptions of me goes back to those first days of polio and what I learned then.

Daddy, my protector, couldn't be there during all the times that I was alone and frightened, when I felt life slipping away or when my lungs lost the strength to pump air anymore. My daddy wasn't there, but he had taught me that God was always with me, would never leave me, and could help when no one else could, and God heard my cries. I knew he was there and that I mattered to him. God loved me and he would see me through, no matter what. He became my other, unlimited "Daddy."

Chapter 4

HOSPITAL LIFE

The days, then the weeks, became seven months in the hospital.

President Franklin D. Roosevelt had founded the National Foundation for Infantile Paralysis (polio) and the March of Dimes campaigns as polio became epidemic in the 1940s and 1950s. Those campaigns paid for everything I and a vast number of polio children needed. All the hospital rooms, treatment, therapy, braces, and other equipment. The amount of money the Polio March of Dimes raised was enormous, especially during the biggest polio epidemic years of 1948 and 1952. On February 15, 1952, the *Spokane Daily Chronicle* carried a front-page article, "$50,030 Raised in Dimes Drive for Polio Fight." That was the dollar number in Spokane County, a mostly rural area. The whole nation responded with similar generosity. Photos from that time of whole wards of people in iron lungs still knot my stomach.

During my polio recovery, two things bolstered my early trust in God. One was the weekly visits from the "Sunday School Lady."

My memory says she was sweetly matronly, but that is the memory of a five-year-old. To have the energy for what she did, she must have been under forty. She was a smile personified. The Sunday School Lady came every week to each room with her flannelgraph board and engagingly told Bible stories. This lady was more than just a welcome chink in the boring hospital routine. She radiated the bubblies. I looked forward to her visits so much that when I gained enough lung power to project my voice and I heard her in a room across the hall, I would holler, "Tell the Sunday School Lady to not forget me!"

As the Sunday School Lady told her stories about Jesus, my trust in God's love and my knowledge of his smile on me became firmly anchored in the Lord's own words in the Bible.

Another way my infant faith sprouted was through the radio. About the time my fingers became strong enough to do my finger crab-crawl so my still-paralyzed arms could reach something, my Aunt Martha gave me a little red radio. At least for 1952, it was little. I still have it. It was ten-by-six-by-six inches and sat on a stand beside my bed. Before long, I learned how to turn the dial and find stations. On Saturdays and Sundays, there were dramatized Bible stories or other child-level Christian programs. I also found the popular radio dramas of the time—*Lone Ranger*, *Fibber McGee and Molly*, *Jack Benny*, and children's programs like *Big Jon* and *Sparkie*. I loved these programs and knew the time and place on the dial for each one.

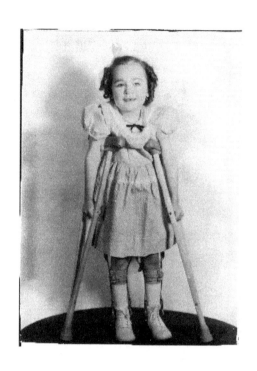

Chapter 5

HOME AGAIN

After seven months in St. Luke's Hospital, I had recovered enough function to go home. I had arrived during a New Year's Day snowstorm, and I left in August heat.

When I was discharged from the hospital, I still couldn't walk, but I could stand with the help of braces from my ribs to my feet. The braces locked at the hips and knees to prop me up, and crutches gave me something to lean on. So though I didn't exactly stand on my own, I thought I did and was so proud I could. The encircling braces looked like a cage but gave me new freedom. I could stand. And at home began to carefully take a few steps.

I loved to join Mom in the kitchen, where she was most of the time. Mom always had the radio in the kitchen tuned to a local station that carried some Christian broadcasts. Besides the broadcasts I had listened to in the hospital, we listened to a favorite of Mom's, *Back to the Bible*. A few months after I came home from the hospital, I was in the kitchen when it came on, and I listened along with Mom. That day the speaker carefully explained that Jesus wanted to clean my heart and live with me. I'm sure I had heard it all before, but that day, added to what I had learned in the hospital from the Sunday School Lady and other broadcasts, what I heard came clear to me. That night, all by myself in my bed, I asked Jesus to do those things. I knew he heard and did, and I began to learn what life with him is. I'm still learning.

My parents continued to take me to physical therapy at St. Luke's hospital until Mr. Carper taught Mom how to do the therapy. I don't know how she managed to fit in two hours of therapy every day along with caring for four other children, cooking, cleaning, laundry, and farm chores. She did, though, and I love her deeply for it.

Dad built a parallel bars ramp off the kitchen porch, where I could practice walking. I was so proud of myself with every step.

A failed experiment was a bright red metal pedal car for me to "drive" on the smooth linoleum floors in the house. Mom and Dad thought that having to pedal would strengthen my legs. Too many gouges and scratches on furniture legs ended that idea. But by then I could walk a bit with my crutches.

Dad heard of a chiropractor in Coeur d'Alene, Idaho, an hour from Spokane, who was doing some innovative things with polio children, so for some months, we drove there every other Saturday. As I remember, it was a biofeedback type of therapy, similar to what Mr. Carper did, trying to enhance the brain-muscle connection. I don't recall much of those sessions except that, like Mr. Carper, the doctor was a kind man.

Before I left the hospital, my parents had agreed to allow me to be nominated for the March of Dimes Poster Child of the next year. Professional photos were taken for that purpose, but that is as far as it went. Soon after I returned home, Mom and Dad wisely withdrew the nomination. Other people questioned that. They were sure I would win not only the county but at least also the state title. After all, my polio had been profound, and—I must admit—I was a cute little girl.

"No," my parents said, "Elinor must not learn to take advantage of her weaknesses to get special attention and favors. She needs to learn to earn what she gets, the same as everyone else."

And so I began to again enter the "real" world.

Chapter 6

REENTRY

Going to the Spokane Interstate Fair each September was a fun family tradition. I could no longer walk it, and though I was small for my age, it would have been difficult for a parent to carry me and watch my siblings, so my parents put me in what we would now call a stroller. That drew looks that embarrassed me. I could tell that the curious stares assumed that I was mentally as well as physically damaged. As if I couldn't even hear, one adult asked my parents what had happened and how I was. She meant well, I suppose, but in my mind, I screamed, "Talk to ME! My legs don't work, but my brain does." That scene is seared in my memory as the time when I began to understand that many people assume that bad legs mean bad brains. I determined to prove that assumption wrong.

I turned six on November 5, 1952, missing the six-by-October 31 cutoff date for entering first grade. This was good because I was not physically able to go to school that soon. I still could not walk more than a few steps.

By the beginning of the next school year, just before I turned seven, I was physically ready to handle going to school. There were no classroom aides nor separate rooms or classes for disabled children. I'm glad that was the case. I was in the normal world of a first grader. I smile when people talk about educational mainstreaming as if it is a new concept.

Getting to my first-grade classroom in Chattaroy Grade School meant going down one small flight of painted cement stairs and up another. With my crutches, I could walk some, but I could not do the stairs. My brother, Ernie, who was in sixth grade then, was the solution to the problem of the steps. He carried me up and down them. Bless him! One wet day he slipped on some water on a step and fell on his back with me on top of him. He hurt his back, but he continued to do that for me. The back injury bothered him into adulthood.

A boy who I now know must have had cerebral palsy also began first grade when I did. I didn't know what his condition was then, but I hoped he could stay. One day, though, he wasn't there and didn't come back. Such things weren't talked about in those days, so no one told us why he left or what his condition was. Instinctively, I knew that at least the other children, if not their parents, too, thought it was because he wasn't smart enough to stay. That reinforced my determination to compete with my brain. By second grade I was one of two at the top of the class. That boy and I became friendly rivals and stayed that way through all twelve grades in our small, rural school district.

By second grade my classmates reinforced a venturesome attitude in me. One morning bad weather wouldn't let us go out for recess, and the teacher trusted us to play quietly in the room while he took an extended break. The class mischief-maker came up with a great activity. He stacked a tower of chairs, one on the other, then asked me, "You want to get on the top one?" Sounded fun! He and other classmates boosted me up, and I was thrilled with the accomplishment. Just then, though, the teacher came back into the room. He saw me on the stack of chairs, blanched white, immediately removed me from pending danger, dismantled the tower, and gave us all what-for. "What a stupid trick! You are all grounded inside all day!" It still makes me grin. I think the teacher assumed I was bullied into climbing up there. Not so! I very happily did it. My friends wanted me to have some fun, and sure enough, I did!

By third grade, I was out of the ribs-to-feet braces and retained a half-leg brace only on my left leg. Hindsight says it was too soon, if not the completely wrong thing to do, but polio rehab was in its scientific infancy. At the time they thought bracing might keep the muscles from regaining as much strength as they otherwise would.

I still couldn't climb stairs, and my brother Ernie was no longer at my school, so a teacher carried me up and down the steps. Outside at recess, I could only stand and watch the other children play, but I enjoyed doing that.

Many fellow polio survivors tell me about the cruel teasing they received, especially during their elementary school years. That never happened to me, and as an adult, I wondered why, until a former classmate told me that there was a "secret" well-known pact among them that if anyone dared to tease me, he or she would have been decked. Again, I am so grateful to them all. Perhaps our rural upbringing in those days instilled a stronger feeling of community.

Though I felt secure in that community and at home, a nightmare I still remember tells me that unconsciously I was unsure of how I would do in the larger world. The nightmare featured Molly.

Molly was a white-faced red cow. She produced very good milk and calves but was the crankiest thing on our farm. Mom and Dad often warned us, "Don't go near Molly. Don't go inside the fence when she's around or might be. Stay away. She'll run at you and stick you with her horns."

I wasn't about to get near Molly! But one night in a dream, I was in the barn alone. Suddenly Molly was there. As only a cow in a dream could do, she reared on her hind legs, scowled, growled, grabbed a pitchfork, and came at me with it. I couldn't move fast enough to get away, and she stabbed me in the stomach. I woke up with a stomachache, breathless, and my heart beating fast in my ears.

I'm not wise enough to know why I still see this dream so clearly in my head. I'm also not astute enough to know what it meant, except that maybe it said what I didn't want to admit—there were things out there in the world that were too strong for me.

Chapter 7

THE "BODY SHOP"

One summer day after third grade, Dad took me to see a farmer somewhere north of us. We sat outside near the farmer's hayfield, surrounded by an aroma I still love. Even now I can feel the soothing warmth of the sun and my dad's lap, his arms easing what could have been an intimidating situation as the farmer looked me over.

This farmer, I learned, was a Shriner. I didn't know what that was, but Dad did. In those days, a Shriner needed to recommend a child as one who should be accepted into the Shriners Hospital for Crippled Children, the fun-looking hospital I had seen through my window in St. Luke's Hospital. My parents wanted to give me every medical advantage possible for me to get stronger, but they could not afford and did not have insurance for the surgeries and therapy I would need as I grew. Shriners Hospitals did those things for free.

"Yes," the farmer said, "I will recommend her, and you should hear from the hospital soon."

I don't remember much about my first examination in the outpatient area, except that it was long. After a discussion with my parents, they all agreed on a plan for me.

"We'll start with her ankles, to make her feet point forward, not outward," the doctor said. "We can't take her until shortly after school begins again though."

I was glad I had only those first two weeks in fourth grade. Everyone feared Mrs. Green (not her real name), the fourth-grade teacher.

"Not one student in my class leaves fourth grade without feeling my paddle," she bragged and started the countdown the first day.

Please, please, I thought, *Just don't attract Mrs. Green's attention for the next two weeks.*

I was the lucky one who got to escape the threat.

I was nine, going on ten years old, but the only bed available for me in Shriners Hospital was a crib in the ward that otherwise held pre-school age children.

Before I was admitted to the hospital, the staff explained to my parents, "We have a schoolroom, part of the Spokane Public School District, where ambulatory children spend normal school hours every day. A few bed patients are wheeled in too. Other children are attended by a teacher who goes from ward to ward, giving assignments, checking work, and hearing recitations."

I had things to read and went to school every day. In Ward Two, the other children were not school age yet. I couldn't talk much with them, but in the schoolroom, I could chat with other students during breaks.

Many of the children in the Shiners Hospital were from out of state and in the hospital for months at a time. Local patients often had lengthy stays too. However, for me, this first time was just a few weeks. I had the operation to put bone blocks in each ankle to straighten them. My legs were casted below the knees and watched for a time before I got to go home with a wheelchair.

Chattaroy Grade School could not accommodate a wheelchair, so I couldn't go to school for the rest of fourth grade. I didn't have to have Mrs. Green. The school made a special allowance for my mother to teach me at home. Mom had graduated from Lewiston Normal School, a teacher's college, now called Lewis-Clark State College, in Lewiston, Idaho. Her teaching license had long expired, but the district said, "We will authorize you to teach Elinor at home with the curriculum Mrs. Green uses."

During that time, I had the other of the only two dreams or nightmares I remember from my childhood. In this dream, a tiger chased me, and I climbed to the lower branches of a tree.

I hope I'm out of his reach!

He stood on his hind legs, clamped his jaw down on my shins, and pulled. The tiger didn't break through the casts on my legs, though, and I hung tightly to the branches. He gave up and left. This time I didn't wake up scared because I had won the contest. The dream just puzzled me.

In hindsight I wonder if my subconscious emotions were adjusting, telling me that the operations ahead of me were going to help me conquer. Who knows? Again, the fact that I remember it so clearly must be significant.

Sometime during that school year, I went back into the hospital to have the casts removed and to have physical therapy to learn how to walk on my new feet.

My original physical assessment had revealed an s-curve in my spine. The doctors had said, "We will need to straighten and fuse her spine eventually, but we don't like to fuse the spine of a girl before puberty."

However, as I recovered the ability to walk after the ankle surgery, they could see that I needed spinal fusion soon.

"Elinor's spine is collapsing into such a severe S that her internal organs are dangerously crowded. We can't delay any longer," doctors said.

It was summer, between my grades four and five. Instead of playing, soon I was back in the hospital. Preparing me for surgery was a long procedure. Nurses and a doctor took me to a room with a table-like device—an empty rectangular frame with a horizontal suspended wide cotton belt that reminded me of the belts that drove equipment attached to Dad's tractor. I was going to lie on the belt.

Someone placed me on the cotton belt. It was only as wide as I was. Someone else fastened a cloth collar-like strap under my chin and a wide strap around my waist. Then the doctor turned a crank, pulling the two devices in opposite directions. It was not at all comfortable. I stared at the ceiling, willing myself to stay calm.

Finally, "OK, that's enough. Her spine is straight," someone said.

Nurses began to put a cast around my trunk, including the belt. When the cast had hardened, someone cut the belt off at head and tail, and the ordeal was over. The cast had to stay that way for three months so my spine and organs could adjust to proper alignment. Plaster encased me from my waist to my chin. It also extended behind my head, so I couldn't even turn it.

I stayed in the hospital for a few weeks so doctors and nurses could see how I adapted to walking with the weight of the cast and my realigned spine. At first, I had to push a chair around for stability. Finally, the doctors said I could go home for three months, then come back for the first surgery.

I had missed a few weeks of outdoor summer play but quickly stepped back into life at home. One reason is that while in the hospital, every day I got a letter from Mom, telling me that Dusty the cat had three kittens, or how fast the calves were growing, or that Dad had cut the hay, or what my brothers were doing. She also gave me news about my friends, news she learned as their Sunday school teacher and learned from their parents. Her stories were short but bright and descriptive. They made me feel that I was still a part of our home routine.

Before long, my cast felt like a normal part of my body. When my spine was ready, the surgeons explained the plan.

"We'll do the fusion in two stages, half the spine at a time. We will leave a few vertebrae free at the top and two at the bottom of the spine to make any eventual pregnancy easier."

I think it was during the first spinal fusion operation that I woke up in the operating room, right in the middle of the procedure. The surgeon was the first to see I was awake, and he swore, "@#&*! Put this kid back to sleep!"

I wasn't scared. All I thought was, *Dr. M., you said bad words!*

During one of my spinal surgeries, I lost a lot of blood. I woke up too early in the recovery room, and when I opened my eyes, I saw above me some bottles dripping blood into me via an IV line.

I better go back to sleep.

Then I heard another child wake up and start to cry. Instinctively, even though fuzzy brained from the ether, I called out to her, "It's OK. You'll get better," to let her know the frightening ordeal would pass. Hers did, and so did mine as we were wheeled back to our wards.

I don't remember much pain after the first fusion surgery, but I sure remember the pain from the second one. After that surgery, anyone's footsteps on the floor vibrated into my back like fiery bolts of electricity. That sensation gradually eased after a few days, and as strange as it may sound, all these experiences taught me that bad times don't last forever; better days always come.

I again wore a heavy body cast for a long, long time, about nine months. Three months while the spine stretched out, three to recover after the first fusion surgery, and three months to heal after the second surgery.

Doctors gradually cut the final cast down over several weeks so my neck could strengthen to hold up my head again and so other muscles could readjust. The neck and behind-the-head piece went first; then they cut off one shoulder "strap" to further lighten the cast. Now you couldn't see the cast under my clothes—if they were loose enough.

I could walk, but I was top-heavy, and the risk of falling at school kept me at home for the first half of fifth grade.

One day during this period, I had on a pair of knit slippers, and I slipped and fell at home. The weight of the body cast fell on my right leg, which was bent under me. I fractured the tibia right under my knee. My parents took me to the Shriners Hospital for treatment.

"It's a greenstick fracture," the doctor said. "It requires traction to pull one side back in place and straighten the bent side. After it is straight, we will cast the leg."

So I was back in the hospital for an unscheduled stay. It took a week to straighten the bone. After that, the leg was wrapped in a cast, and I had to learn to walk once again. Yes, walk. The cast went all the way down my leg, but they did not cast the foot. That way I could walk with it. I was still in the body cast, so now three-fourths of my body was in casts, but I was still walking!

I still couldn't physically handle Chattaroy Grade School though. The school district had anticipated that, so they got a grant from the state to send Mr. Wells, the fifth-grade teacher, to my house twice a week after school to give me the same work his class was doing and to check my assignments. Mom guided my work in the meantime. By the second semester, my casts were off and I was able to join my classmates at school, right in sync with where they were.

My last operation was to straighten both knees, which had developed a bad valgus, or "knock-kneed" deformity, possibly because I had not worn braces for several years. So after seventh grade, I was once again in the Shriners Hospital for about three months, which was my average stay each time. After the surgery, I learned for the nth time to walk on my "new" legs. This time, though, it was clear that I needed braces to hold the bones and joints where they belonged. My weak muscles couldn't do that.

I knew that when I left the hospital this time, it would be the last time, and I was sad. There had been a lot of pain and struggle in those years but also a lot of fun with girls who were going through similar things. Even now my mind grins at the memories.

Chapter 8

MY EXPANDING WORLD

I loved the two teachers in the school at Shriners Hospital. Both ladies' smiles and energy showed that they loved teaching there. They handled grades one through eight, and maybe kindergarten, too—I don't remember. The hospital population was small, so they did not have many students. There were two "big boy" wards with five beds each, and the same for "big girls." There was one ward for babies, one for preschoolers, and one divided ward of two private rooms for patients who needed to be by themselves. That was where I was after I broke my leg because that was the only place where there was an empty bed.

In the classroom, there was immediate access to the teacher. I liked that, but I also liked staying in the ward to do my schoolwork, with occasional check-ups by the teacher who made rounds. Either way, it was individual study, which suited me well.

One memory of my time in the schoolroom was when I memorized part of "The Song of Hiawatha," the poem by Henry Wadsworth Longfellow. It took me, in my mind, to where I longed to be able to wander again at home. The opening words immediately pulled me in.

> By the shores of Gitche Gumee,
> By the shining Big-Sea-Water,
> Stood the wigwam of Nokomis,
> Daughter of the Moon, Nokomis.
> Dark behind it rose the forest,
> Rose the black and gloomy pine-trees,
> Rose the firs with cones upon them.

The word picture Longfellow painted put me back among the pine and fir trees of the woods around our farm at home. Places I loved to explore.

Dad and Mom owned three unconnected pieces of acreage where Dad grew hay and cows. The piece where our house was also held the barn and other outbuildings. That piece of land had forty acres of open field and forty acres of woods next to several hundred acres of woods owned by others. Woods surrounded the fields on three sides. The fourth side was next to our uncle's farm field. Our house was only 200 feet from the west end of the property and the woods beyond. The east end of the field was a hill that met the woods.

A forester by training and a range manager by career, it seemed Dad knew every inch of those woods and fields. He would invite us children to walk through them with him and try to teach us what the plants were, how to recognize the difference between species, and even their scientific names. I wish I could remember all that!

Until my later teens, I couldn't walk with Dad up the hill on the east end of the field and into the woods there. Before then, when Dad took the tractor into the woods to cut firewood, thin trees, pick wild berries, or hunt mushrooms, I rode on the tractor with him. I may not have absorbed Dad's knowledge of everything in the woods, but I did absorb his love of the woods, the fields, and the animals they held. "The Song of Hiawatha" spoke to that part of me.

But I wasn't there. I was in the Shriners Hospital, where I knew I was gaining the physical ability to enjoy my home environment even more than before.

All of us in the Shriners Hospital, whether we were in school or on our beds, dressed each day in hospital-issue regular clothes, girls in dresses and boys in slacks. No hospital gowns. Our attire was plain, but things felt less hospitalish that way.

There was no Sunday school lady as there had been at St. Luke's Hospital. I missed church and Sunday school. During one of my stays in a big girls' ward when I was twelve, I asked my parents,

"Could you bring me a couple of Sunday school study guides from our church so I can teach Sunday school for some of the girls in my ward?" At least one ward-mate joined my "class." I loved doing that each Sunday morning. I loved teaching, period. Mom once told me, "When you were little, you used to line up your little brothers and your dolls to be your class so you could play you were the teacher."

A few years before I taught my tiny hospital Sunday school class, I started to sense that God wanted me to be a missionary one day. It was just a tiny, unformed inkling, and it wasn't on my mind as I taught. I was just having fun.

My many-week stays at the Shriners Hospital became part of missionary training in another way too. The era of tightly restricted parental hospital visits was still in place. The rule at the Shrine, all the years I was there, was two visiting hours on Sunday afternoons only. And of course, there were no public-access phones. I was learning to happily fill my days apart from my family. This wasn't without daily news though. I don't know how my mother did it, but she wrote and mailed a letter to me every day—as if she didn't have enough to do! As before, I knew what kind and how many mushrooms Dad found in the woods and how good they tasted. I learned when Dad got a new batch of baby chickens, when and how many kittens Buffy had, which cow had a calf, what my sister and brothers were doing—maybe even how many grasshoppers they caught that day. Anything to fill a home-newsy page. What love!

Leading one or two girls through each week's Sunday school lesson didn't equate to my being angelic. My best friend during one of my stays was a girl I'll call FunGal because I can't remember her name and she was great fun. FunGal was not of the 99 percent of patients who were there for polio-related issues. She was there to try to get better use of an arm that was withered due to improper casting after it was broken. Her legs and one arm worked fine. And she loved risky thrills. As often as we could, we would get an abandoned wheelchair. I sat in it, and FunGal pushed it with her good arm. We would peek down the hall to make sure no nurses were watching, then FunGal ran as fast as she could, pushing me down the hall, and at the very end of the run gave one side of the wheelchair a nudge to make it spin around. Wow, was that fun! I didn't ever tip over either.

During another stay, my best friend was the girl in the next bed. She was Japanese, and every Sunday her parents brought her a Japanese treat. She especially loved dried squid snacks.

"Would anyone like to try some?" she offered.

I was the only girl who ever accepted the offer, and I liked them! It was my first introduction to the adventure of ethnic food. Even though I was stuck in a hospital, my world was expanding through the friends I met there.

In those days, Shriners Hospital permanently discharged patients at the age of fourteen. I was sad when that happened. Yes, "The Shrine" was associated with a lot of pain, discomfort, and the hard work of learning how to use my "new" body after each surgery, but it was also in many ways a happy time.

Chapter 9
WHICH PATH?

The operations were a great help, but I knew that God sometimes fixes bodies without doctors.

After my first operation and before the spinal fusions, a certain famous faith healer came to Spokane, set up a tent, and held healing meetings. My parents were very skeptical, but after the pressure of several times hearing, "Well, don't you want to give your daughter a chance to be healed?" they relented and took me to a meeting.

When the time came for people to line up for healing, someone helped me get in the line, and at my turn, the preacher put his hands on my head and pronounced me healed. But my body felt no different. The preacher's staff showed me and others who were chosen for photos for the "healer's" magazine where to go for the pictures. As I walked to that area of the tent, I tripped and fell in the thick sawdust. I got up and stood where they told me. Someone manually leveled my shoulders (my curving spine had made them uneven), and they took the photo. I would go in the magazine as one who was healed in Spokane. I knew it was all a lie. Despite what they said, my body was no different.

Other polio survivors relate similar experiences, and it left them wary or even bitter toward "religion." It didn't do that to me. Why? Maybe because I already knew God for myself. I read the Bible almost daily and knew that people can be—well, frankly, deceivers. But God is not.

I wanted to be healed though, and knew God could do it. I pictured in my mind getting on the school bus the next morning by myself, not needing the driver to carry me up the steps. With this on my mind, a day or two later I stood at the bottom of the steps leading up to my bedroom and asked God about it.

Just think—if you did that, wouldn't the other kids be surprised?! They would all know you are real then. Why don't you?

I don't know how, but I knew God answered with "Not yet." That was enough. I went up the stairs satisfied. I still am, even though I may not be healed until I reach heaven.

In the meantime, from first grade through high school, my family compensated for what I couldn't do. Getting to the school bus, for instance, was a quarter-mile hike up a dirt road—not possible for me. My great-uncle Carl, who had been a Boeing engineer, made a rickshaw-type wheelchair for me. It made having to use a wheelchair fun. It had bicycle and airplane tires for smooth riding to the bus stop on the gravel road. Long handles projected out front so brothers Harlow and Dick could easily pull the chair.

By my sixth grade, Harlow and Dick grew strong enough to pedal a bike with a passenger, and I became able to balance sideways on the seat on the back of a bike. We handled the bus stop trips that way. When the rickshaw was not needed for that anymore, we used it for play. Things like riding in it while a brother pushed it so fast it almost tipped on tight corners. Fun! In the winter, when there was snow and ice on the road, Harlow and Dick pulled me on a sled to the bus stop.

After I had the knee surgeries, I again had full-leg braces as well as crutches and could walk much better, though not long distances yet. I soon turned thirteen and knew for sure that being a missionary was my future. Our family attended the only church in Chattaroy. The small congregation of farm families held a prayer meeting on Wednesday evenings. It was typically not heavily attended, but one weekly meeting was an exception. A missionary speaker would be there, so more people came that night—about thirty. I was among them.

The guest speaker was a man from China whose broken English indicated his origins and whose physical appearance confirmed what he told us of severe malnutrition in his village during his childhood. His legs were bowed, his stomach protruded, and so did his teeth. He told us that living conditions in his village changed when missionaries brought the message of Jesus to them, and most of the villagers believed. They no longer needed to give large amounts of their food crops to the idols or profits from crops to buying opium, so they were better nourished.

The speaker pled with our handful of farm families to see God's heartbeat for the people of the world who did not yet know Jesus. Then, of all things, he asked, "If anyone here feels God wants you to be a missionary, would you step up to the front here and say so openly?" What a thing to ask of this audience of farm families. No one there could accept such an invitation. Except one. Me. I felt it was time to let my church family know what I knew in my heart. My stomach tightened, hoping the people there would understand.

I retrieved my crutches from under the pew in front of me and walked down the short aisle. As I did, I saw embarrassment in the eyes of the adults. I saw they were thinking, *Oh, dear, this little girl doesn't know what she is doing.* I became embarrassed, knowing this looked like a foolish goal, and that made me look foolish.

Over thirty-five years later, Ormel, the only man who had been there and was not already in heaven, told me what happened after the service. He said that one of the men apologized to the speaker that the only person who had responded to his invitation was that "poor little crippled girl" who could never achieve such a goal.

As Ormel related this, he asked me, "You want to know what the speaker said to that?"

"Yes, please."

"That dear Chinese man said, 'Whom the Lord calls, he will use.'"

I knew nothing of that conversation at the time though. All I knew was that I was embarrassed. I felt I had made a fool of myself.

That God had made me look foolish because he was the one behind it all. I determined that I was never going to be seen as ridiculous again.

I tried to shove my commitment to missionary work to the back of my mind through the rest of my secondary school years. I had been discharged from the care of the Shriners Hospital when I was fourteen, and I was full of confidence.

I know what I can and can't do, and I'm smart enough to figure out a reasonable career for myself.

At the same time, though, I wanted to live consistently with what I understood life with Jesus to be. Did I truly think that rebellion and obedience can co-exist? My only excuse is that teenagers don't always think straight. The day would come when I would have to choose one path or the other.

Chapter 10
MY CHOICE

In our small school district, there were two elementary schools and one high school. The two elementary schools were grades one through seven, and the district's combined eighth grade had a room in the high school. This meant that half of my new eighth-grade class would not know me. Would I be accepted or teased? I decided to take my cue from Proverbs 18:24: "A man that hath friends must shew himself friendly." Ignoring the stares and cold shoulders, I was purposely friendly toward everyone, even smiling when I didn't feel like it. It worked. Before long I was accepted by all.

By the time I reached high school age, I could walk well though slowly and with frequent pauses to rest. When school was out for the summer, one thing I loved to do in the morning was put half a sandwich and a Gideon New Testament (with Psalms, Proverbs, and hymns) in my pockets, call to my dog Sparkie, and head off for a day in the woods. Even though I was still wearing leg braces and using crutches, I walked two miles or so before returning home in the late afternoon.

First, I headed for two large ponds in the middle of the woods that neighbors (in the rural sense) owned to the north and up a hill. They called the ponds Evergreen Lakes, which we privately laughed at. They were ever green all right, especially in summer, when one was covered by algae. There I ate my sandwich, read, sang, talked to God, and lay down for a while in the warm sun. The sounds of the birds, the wind in the pine trees, the trees creaking as they swayed, scolding pine squirrels—all mixed with the sharp scent of pine, the sweet wildflowers, the musty smell of hot drying leaves and pine needles, and the brackish odor of the ponds. It was all so soothing. I loved it.

Lunch and rest over, Sparkie and I explored old logging trails in the woods behind the fields until I had to head back home for dinner. Sometimes that meant going cross-country down wooded hills in the general direction of our house. Sparkie, a Sheltie mix, was handy to have along. She took the deer trails, so I followed her and always came out where I needed to be.

It didn't dawn on me at the time, but looking back now, I wonder how Mom let me do that without ever protesting that I might get hurt or lost. I don't remember either of my parents ever saying, "Oh, honey, I don't think you can do __ [whatever]." Instead, they silently let me try any crazy idea I had and discover for myself whether I could do it or not. Maybe partly because they knew I would try it anyway. I remember Mom teasing me with, "You are so stubborn!" I always replied, "No, Mom, I'm just focused."

During those years, my inner contradiction between rebellion and obedience to God persisted. When I was a high school junior, my dad and our pastor took me and a friend up to Three Hills, Alberta, Canada, to visit Prairie Bible Institute, a well-known missionary training school. What gave them the idea to take us way up there and to that school I don't know. Maybe Dad remembered that Wednesday night a few years earlier when I responded to the impossible-for-me invitation of the Chinese speaker, and Dad wanted to give it a chance.

What impressed me at that visit was how unadorned the dorm rooms were. Austere might be a better word. I also saw how regimented everything was, how no-nonsense the Bible classes were, and that the men and women students ate on different sides of the dining room. Not by choice—it was the rule. There was no idle contact between male and female students. "Training disciplined soldiers for Christ," was the school's motto. Not mine. I was still in the "I am smart enough to figure this out myself" mode.

When we came back from that visit to Prairie Bible Institute (PBI) and people asked me how I liked it, I said, "It was nice enough to visit, but I wouldn't ever want to go there."

Toward the middle of my senior year of high school, I began to experiment with using less walking assistance. First, I disengaged the locks on my braces that held my knees straight when I stood. Could I stand without locks and my knees not buckle? Yes, I could. And could I also walk that way? Yes. Then I removed the braces to see how I did. I thought I did well, so I asked my parents to make an appointment with the orthopedic surgeon who had done most of the work on me at the Shriners Hospital. Would he agree that it would be fine for me to stop using braces?

On the day of the appointment, Dr. M. asked me to take off my braces and walk around the exam room. I did, and he said, "At this stage, many patients decide whether to use just braces or just crutches. If you want to take off the braces and use only crutches, you can." Then he said what I didn't expect. "But from what we know of your bone structure and muscle strength, you should not be able to walk this well."

At that moment, it was as if only God and I were in that room—as if he put his hand on my head and told me he was making a way for me to follow his plans for me. His missionary plans that I had publicly committed to. But I had a choice to make. I could obey or drop the whole thing and walk away from him.

Over the next two weeks, I struggled with what I would do. I was just a few weeks from high school graduation and was already accepted by Whitworth College (now Whitworth University) in Spokane. I knew, though, that saying yes to God meant going to PBI instead for concentrated missionary training, something that would seem a foolish choice to many. They would think of Whitworth as a good choice, but Prairie—not really. I knew, though, that I could not have it both ways. I either had to follow God's way or stop pretending to. I could not straddle the paths of obedience and rebellion.

One day, as my internal war continued, I read Psalm 143. Verse 10 in the King James Version I used at the time said, "Teach me to do thy will; for thou art my God: thy spirit is good; lead me into the land of uprightness." The New International Version says, "Teach me to do your will, for you are my God; may your good Spirit lead me on level ground." I understood that I didn't have to be fully cheerful about doing what I knew God wanted; I just needed to be willing to be taught that it was a happy thing.

So I was frank with God. "I am afraid of being made to look foolish by aiming for something impossible," I said, "but you are my God. Teach me to do your will. I will take the first step and let you take care of what happens."

As best as I could, not knowing totally what was happening within me, I confided to my parents, "I believe God wants me to go to PBI, not Whitworth." Did they doubt that? I don't know, but I do know that they encouraged me: "If that is the case, honey, that is what you should do."

By now it was getting late to apply to colleges. I quickly applied to Prairie and was accepted on physical probation. Winters in northern Alberta are usually very snowy, with frequent strong winds. I might not be able to handle walking around campus in those conditions, but they would let me try for one semester and see if I could.

Just a few short weeks after I decided to go to PBI, fifty of us graduated from Riverside High School, the largest class up until then. Not only was I proud that I marched up the aisle without braces, just with crutches, but also the broad smiles from my class-mates said they were proud of me too. I could feel the smile of my whole rural community. In a way, leaving my braces behind was as significant a "graduation" as the academic one.

I had little idea of the challenges ahead.

Chapter 11

TO THE SNOWY NORTH

After PBI accepted me, they sent a list of dorm room items that I would need to bring. Scatter rug, wardrobe curtains, washstand curtain, window curtains, bedding, and other basics. The rooms were bare-bones simple. They also sent a ribbon of tiny laundry ID tags to cut apart and sew onto every item of anything that would need to be laundered. During the months between high school graduation and PBI, Mom and I spent every minute we could stitching those on—by hand, of course; they were too small to do by machine. Besides sewing on the labels, I made sure the clothes I planned to take fit Prairie's strict dress code. No slacks. Skirts and dresses below the knees by five inches and sleeves below the elbows. It was a type of boot camp designed to do as the motto said, "Training disciplined soldiers for Christ."

In my mind, I dismissed the physical probation thing. I was still in the world-by-the-tail mode and full of confidence that I could do anything I set my mind on. I had decided that I was going to be at PBI for only one year anyway. I would take some good Bible classes, then go on to "real" college.

PBI let me know that there was a student in Spokane who was willing to give two other students a ride up north to school. Her name was JoAnn. I decided to accept her offer. This was JoAnn's second year, so she was a handy resource for advice on how to prepare. She also had rules of her own. Millie (JoAnn's other passenger) and I could take only one suitcase each, of a certain maximum size because that was all the room she had in her car, and it was all any of us would need anyway—according to JoAnn. Somehow Mom, Dad, and I managed to fit a small rug, curtains, bedding, clothes, and one special stuffed animal into one suitcase. JoAnn laughed at the stuffed animal. "You're not a baby anymore," she said. Gruff? Well, I grew to love JoAnn with her no-nonsense mind and huge heart. She became not only my means of transportation but also my sentinel. She kept close (but not too close) track of how things were with me so she could step in to help if needed. What a friend!

Within a day or two of arriving on campus, I met with Mr. Pulliam, my assigned advisor, to plan my class schedule. He immediately reminded me of Uncle Carl, Mom's uncle, and our substitute grandpa whom we all loved, the one who had made me the unique wheelchair years before. Mr. Pulliam had the same kind smile and twinkle in his eye that Uncle Carl had. Same mustache and sparse hair too. I told him to draw up a one-year plan because I would be at PBI for only that long. Mr. Pulliam looked me in the eye with that soft twinkle and said, "Oh, I believe the Lord always finishes what he starts. Now let's work out your four-year plan and choose your classes for this year."

Utterly disarmed, I said no more as Mr. Pulliam outlined my first year of four. How could I argue with "The Lord always finishes what he starts"? I walked back to my dorm wondering what had just happened.

Chapter 12

LOTS TO LEARN

Of the two girls' dorms, mine was the farthest from the center of campus because it was the one that did not have steps at the entrance. It was a long way from Mr. Pulliam's office. As I crutched my way down the flower-lined sidewalk, the faint aroma of lively petunias, marigolds, snapdragons, and others combined to soothe my swirling thoughts. Those flowers helped soften my soul to accept the change to my one-year plan. So did the clean breeze that blew off the ripe hay and grain on the prairies. I was in the right place.

When I got back to my dorm and JoAnn came to ask me how my appointment with Mr. Pulliam went, she chuckled when I told her what he said. She replied, "Then God's telling you to drop your old idea and settle down and study. Do it."

I did.

As in high school, not having to take physical education meant an extra slot for an academic subject. That caused more homework than most students had. Despite that I also signed up for orchestra, playing my cornet. That was my relaxation. To my delight, I found that as the only female trumpet player, I had to sit with the guys. I missed my brothers' male ways more than I thought I would. Being among guys in the orchestra helped me feel at home.

I was embarrassed that my English grammar diagnostic test put me in the lowest English class. The Canadian terms for aspects of grammar were not what we used in my little high school. Frequently, I had no clue what the exam question was about. If the question was a fill-in-the-blank type, many times the word I supplied was not the expected one. As a result, my score on the placement exam put me near the bottom of the stack. They enrolled me in the lowest English class, among students from non-English speaking countries. I caught on to the Canadian terms quickly, though, and was soon—and sadly—promoted to a different class. I loved the cultural differences and accent flavors of that bottom-level group. Those international students added a delightful sparkle to life that I would miss.

I soon came to love the search question method used in all Bible and doctrine classes. We were required to study one and a half hours per class session, answering the study questions for the next session. We did not have textbooks and were not allowed to use commentaries or other aids besides a concordance—just our Bible. Cross-references were OK, but we were honor-bound to not read any explanatory notes on the pages of our Bibles. Sometimes we got only one question, and that one took the whole one-and-a-half hours to research and answer. What a gift that kind of study was to me. It taught me how to think biblically—to see accurately what a text said and how its principle was confirmed and expanded by other Scripture passages. It is the basis of how I think through verses and sections of the Bible even now.

The classroom was not the only place of great learning though. I also learned from watching the lives of faculty and staff. One who stands out in my mind was Mr. Koch, the main groundskeeper. He kept the grounds looking good in the warm seasons, and the sidewalks clear of snow and ice in the winter. Steam tunnels ran under the sidewalks, and that helped to keep the snow mostly melted off, but sometimes it just melted into ice. Even now, in my mind, I can see myself leaving the dorm before most everyone, and there was Mr. Koch in front of the girls' dorms, tears frozen on his cheeks from the icy wind, clearing the sidewalks. Joy radiated from his frost-red face. That taught me more about what it means to be the Lord's servant than any classroom lecture.

I was on the sidewalk earlier than most in the mornings because my campus job required I be in the dining hall before other students. Everyone had a campus job to help with tuition, and mine was to keep a record of the women students as they entered the dining hall before each meal. Skipping meals was not allowed without permission.

That first year at PBI, as autumn moved into winter, the trees changed their clothing from leaves to thick, beautiful hoarfrost such as I had never seen. I had also never seen snow as dry as the blowing snow of the Canadian prairies. My crutches acted as struts against being blown over by the Chinook winds. I was glad I had crutches as I watched other girls get bowled over by strong gusts.

At the end of the first semester, the dean of women called me to her office. "You are no longer on probation," she said. "We see that you can handle getting around campus fine, even in the snow."

It took a moment for me to catch what she said. I had taken all that so much in stride I had forgotten I was on physical probation.

The end of that first semester also marked other vital changes. As I took each day one at a time and did what I knew God wanted me to do, I discovered that obeying him was a joyful thing. Fear that I might look foolish, no matter what God asked me to do, was gone. If things seemed imprudent, God would handle them. Also gone was any thought of not continuing at PBI through graduation. I happily looked forward not only to finishing but also to the process of getting there.

My roommate during my first semester was Wilma, a quiet sophomore. If she saw some of my inner struggles, she didn't offer advice, but she did smile approval at each positive step I took.

As winter took hold, Wilma developed a respiratory illness so strong that she had to go to the infirmary. She got permission to try to attend some classes but had such a loud whoop-like cough that I feared she could not get well. She did finally have to drop out of school and return to her home.

At the beginning of the second semester, the empty bed in my room was filled by a gal enrolled in pre-freshman preparatory classes. She had, I discovered, deep emotional problems that negatively shaped how she behaved. My naivete thought I just needed to change how I approached her, but nothing worked. I finally went to the women's dean about how this girl was physically rough with me—sometimes even locked me out of the room, and sometimes spoke to me in strange ways that I sensed were inappropriate. As a result, the dean investigated the situation, and this gal was sent home.

I also have nonspecific memories of another difficult-to-get-along-with roommate, but she also left before the end of the semester, and no one else was placed with me. Frankly, I enjoyed being alone. From the second half of my sophomore year through the rest of my time at PBI, I was a floor counselor (commonly called a resident assistant, or RA). The best perk was a room to myself. As I reflected on my roommate experiences, I saw how the Lord used them to prepare me to try to help the girls put in my charge. Just as Wilma had been patient with my spiritual struggles without judgment, I similarly tried to discern the difference between bitter rebellion and the occasional "naughtiness" of a girl whose heart God was molding. I loved watching that process. I had also learned a bit about deep emotional damage and about conflict that I was not responsible for nor able to resolve.

Chapter 13

TOOLS FOR MY SKILL BUCKET

My favorite teacher was Mr. Alban Douglas, who taught the missions classes. He and his wife, Anna, had been missionaries in China. After WWII, when the communists were taking control and trying to erase Christianity, the Douglases were under house arrest in west China. Mrs. Douglas went into a coma with eclampsia—a dangerous complication of pregnancy—and their first baby was stillborn. Mr. Douglas put the red-headed girl into a box, went into their backyard, dug a grave, and buried her there. The emotional and spiritual honesty with which Mr. Douglas spoke about this and other experiences gave credibility to everything else he said.

But his style was not glum. Whatever Mr. Douglas presented, whether principles gleaned from his own experiences or Scripture, he did so with a radiant face and full energy. He didn't merely gesture. His body contorted as if boneless as he mimed the stories. Mr. Douglas's gravelly voice added even more drama. He lubricated his throat with the Vic's cough drops always in his cheek. No one slept through his classes.

One story is especially vivid in my mind. Mr. Douglas talked about being in China on a river sampan with way more people than it should have held, as usual. Night fell, and everyone prepared to sleep on the deck of the boat, side by side, one person's head next to another's feet to save space.

"I hated it," Mr. Douglas said. "I disliked the Chinese and their crude ways. I had no love for them at all. I did not want to be there, was angry that I was, and told God so. In the night air, I became cold and had no blanket. Suddenly, a Chinese man offered for me to cuddle up with him in his blanket—which I accepted. When I woke up the next morning, all the prejudice I had against the Chinese was gone. I realized that they, too, had something to offer me."

Then he stopped, looked at us, and asked, "So why did I stay? Not because of my new regard for the Chinese, but because I loved God and knew that he loved them. God gave me love for the Chinese as I asked him to do, but love for a culture or people is neither a correct nor good enough motivation for missions. Love for God must be the core. He will eventually give you love for the people he sends you to, but only love for God—first—can sustain you."

Maybe God burned that lesson on my mind because he knew what lay years ahead of me.

My music classes and ensembles also added fun to my PBI years. For the first two or three years, I was the only girl in the trumpet section of the orchestra. And I was always at least second chair. Not only was being around guys refreshing, so was the fun of making music. It was a happy break from the brain-strain of my classes. We were the largest college orchestra in western Canada, so when we put on concerts in Calgary and Edmonton in their Jubilee auditoriums, it was always a well-attended big deal. We traveled to and from those concerts by bus, which gave a privileged social outlet. We kept the rules—women and men sat separately, but oversight relaxed, and we laughed and talked a lot.

Mr. Snyder finished his music teaching career at the end of my sophomore year. The next year Mr. Paul Rausch came. He was able to show with his mouth shape and his voice the sound he wanted from us and the method we should use to produce it. And he did it with sparkle and joy. Mr. Rausch pulled a level of music out of us we didn't know we had in us. One of the unique things he put together was a trumpet sextet. I auditioned and became one of the six. Again, I was the only girl and by far the shortest player. My size was a problem because we always stood in line to play. The guys were from five feet, ten inches tall and up. I was four feet, seven-and-a-half inches—mainly by inheritance and shortened a bit by polio. The height uniformity problem was solved by the school's woodshop. They made me a nice-looking block of wood to stand on. It was about ten inches high. When it came time for the trumpet sextet to play, we walked up to our line, and two of the guys helped me step onto my wooden block. We settled, raised our trumpets, and began to play.

Another new musical group Mr. Rausch led was the brass choir. Brass players auditioned for this select group. From the main group, Mr. Rausch chose an even smaller group to travel for a few weeks after school finished for the summer. We represented the school as we played in churches, gymnasiums—any venue large enough for our ensemble. PBI did not have money for us to stay in hotels, so we stayed in the homes of people who volunteered to have us. Often this meant rural homes. That was familiar to me, of course, but one home in Montana was more than ordinarily rural. We girls got to stay in the house—on simple slab beds in the unfinished attic. The boys stayed in the barn and slept on the hay. The stories told on the bus the next morning were amusing, for sure.

The varied experiences of traveling with the PBI brass choir helped to show me that life can be lived in a number of ways. We don't need comforts like beds and mattresses or conveniences like electricity or modern appliances. Those things are nice but don't in themselves bring happiness.

The music tour ended, summer ended, and school began again with a new lineup of classes.

Homiletics stands out in my mind. I enjoyed writing, speaking, and teaching and was tolerably good at those things, but the semester opened with the theory of preaching and biblical exposition, rather than practice. My brain was not ready to navigate such dry, confusing concepts. I tried, but with little success, and my homework and test scores were pitiful. That was a blow to my ego. Fortunately, the actual preaching part of the class rescued my overall grade.

Most important, though, was learning how to construct a Bible lesson from the passage and supporting passages without heavy reliance on commentaries. Though in this class we could use commentaries, their use was limited. That restriction reinforced the biblical thinking principles that the Bible classes taught. I cannot overstate how those principles became the permanent fabric of how I think and reason even now.

It might seem strange, then, that somewhere during my third or fourth year I had an unexpected crisis of belief. I don't know what brought it on. It wasn't because of anything I read or heard or anything else. I simply realized I didn't believe anything the teachers said. *Look at all these students. Believing it all,* my mind said. *How could they be so gullible?*

What was I to do about this? Pray? To a god I didn't believe in? However, in case he did exist, I said, "God, if you are real, and are truly there, show me somehow that you are."

I don't know how that crisis resolved itself any more than I know what brought it on. But I know that, with time, God—who is real and was there after all—did what I asked of him. I became more than intellectually convinced that he is real and Scripture is true. This conviction was now my own—not borrowed from parents, teachers, or anyone else. It was between God and me alone. The change was profound. It produced a whole new dimension of relationship with God and his Word. I had a new, active, joyful interaction with God about everything, including all the surprising adventures he would bring my way.

Chapter 14

BIGGER CHALLENGES

I had never traveled alone before, but this time I had no choice if I wanted to go to my brother Harlow's wedding. I got permission to take some days off school, but my only travel choice was to fly from Calgary to Spokane and back. The flight to Spokane was fun and went well with no problems, but going back to school, the plane was late arriving in Calgary. I missed my ride to Three Hills, and I had almost no money with me. I phoned the school, and they told me to take a cab to the YWCA, stay there the night, and the next morning walk the block to the train station and take the train to Three Hills.

The cabby must have known I had little money because he refused a tip. That left me just enough for the night at the Y and the train fare. But none for food that night nor the next morning. I lay on my bunk listening to the chatter of some girls playing cards on their bunks in the dim light and wondered how my strength would be the next day. It held out. I walked the block to the train station, found my seat on the train, and enjoyed the scenery of the prairie fields we passed.

When the train stopped at Three Hills, someone met me there, and soon I was back on the familiar PBI campus, just in time for my first-hour class. Was I ever hungry for lunch after the morning classes! But the Lord had shown me that things might take me by surprise, but they would not change his care of me. *He's got it all worked out ahead of time. I can trust him for that.* What an important lesson that would be for my future.

Another event taught me about trusting God in the unexpected, though at the time I had no idea how it would one day figure in my future. Shortly into my senior year, we students gathered at the auditorium for a special meeting. There a faculty member told us, "We just heard that Prairie graduate, Phil Masters, and his fellow-missionary, Stan Dale, along with some tribal evangelists were killed."

Stan and Phil were missionaries to tribes that neighbor each other in the mountains of Irian Jaya, Indonesia (now Papua, Indonesia). Stan worked with the Yali tribe and Phil with the next tribe east, the Kimyals. On September 25, 1968, they walked through Yali territory in an area where the local group of Yalis wanted nothing to do with the gospel. Yali men there shot Stan and Phil full of arrows, killing them. Phil's death left behind his wife, Phyliss, also a PBI alum, their four children, and an unborn child.

The shock of the reality of what being a missionary might mean sobered the campus. I had not the slightest clue then that I would one day work among the same Kimyal people at Korupun where Phil and Phyliss had worked.

Chapter 15

PRACTICAL PREPARATION

Sometime during my first year at Prairie, a representative of Child Evangelism Fellowship (CEF) came to campus to recruit students to a summer of mission work, holding backyard Five Day Clubs all summer throughout that representative's state. The idea intrigued me. I wondered if CEF in Washington State had a program like that.

I found an address for CEF of Washington State, wrote to them, and found out that yes, they did have a summer missionary program for Bible college students. I filled out the application they sent, mailed it, and by return mail learned that I could go to training camp the coming summer. If my assessment after camp went well, they would assign me a ministry partner, and we would get our summer itinerary.

Training camp was no shoo-in. We had to almost memorize the story script for all five days of both the Bible story and the missionary story that we would use that summer. *My brain can't hold all this!* I often thought as I went off alone under some tree on the campground to practice and practice until the stories stayed in my head and flowed out my mouth. We also had to learn the memory verses and the memorization games that went with them. When I got my completion and acceptance certificate at the end of camp, I knew I had earned it. I was assigned a partner, and we set out on the summer's adventure. First, we drove to the CEF Washington State headquarters in Yakima. There each team got their schedule of places, host homes, and dates. Office staff and volunteers made sure we had maps, showed us routes and spots, prayed over us, and with a bit of nervousness, we set out.

I spent my summers this way during all four of my years at PBI. I don't remember two of my summer partners. However, Ginny, my partner for two years, and I are still in touch. Ginny, also a student at PBI, was one year ahead of me and aimed to be a missionary after she graduated. We worked well together, enjoyed each other, and took equal responsibility for sending our reports and otherwise communicating with the state CEF office. Our clubs were in back-yards and parks, itinerant farm-worker camps, people's homes, and small churches as their Vacation Bible School program.

We drove from town to town across the state in Ginny's car, one her dad made sure was roadworthy. He may have shaken his head, though, at the rod attached above the back seat, the whole span of which held our clothes for the summer. Girls! We loved to sing together as we went down the road and to practice the Scripture memory passage we chose for the summer. To this day I see a stretch of road in my mind when I hear Psalm 34.

> I will bless the Lord at all times: his praise shall
> continually be in my mouth.
> My soul shall make her boast in the Lord: the humble
> shall hear thereof, and be glad.
> O magnify the Lord with me, and let us exalt his
> name together.
> I sought the Lord, and he heard me, and delivered me
> from all my fears. (Psalm 34:1–4)

Sometimes our host in the town where we were assigned had already distributed the invitations to the Five Day Club that would be in their backyard. Sometimes we had to do that on a Sunday afternoon in the neighborhood near a city park where we would begin the club the next morning. We did the same for the afternoon club in another park. We always had two or three ninety-minute clubs a day. The first day of each club started with the song, "Jesus Loves Me." Most children knew that song, so it gave us something familiar to start with. But we had kids from all kinds of home backgrounds. One morning as we held the club on a patch of a grassy hill in a farm migrant camp, a young boy began yelling, twitching, and rolling down the hill. It wasn't a seizure. It was the first time I had personally seen demon possession. Our mission classes at PBI had taught us the reality of such a situation and what to do. We stopped and prayed, the boy became calm, and the club returned to normal.

Another time, as we drove into a city that had a reputation for occult practices, Ginny said, "Do you feel the darkness as I do?"

Yes, I did. It was like driving under and into a blanket of smog. An almost tangible heaviness. The next morning, we started the club as we always did: "Let's sing the song 'Jesus Loves Me.'" A five-year-old raised his hand. "Yes, Davy?" Ginny said. Davy was excited. "I know who Jesus is! My daddy saw him last week in a séance."

Ginny and I glanced at each other for a split second, hoping the other had a good response. One of us explained, "But this isn't talking about that Jesus. This song is about Jesus, God's Son," and went on to explain who he truly is. Then we sang "Jesus Loves Me."

All experiences, the difficult and the joyful ones, were great preparation for our future missionary careers.

Chapter 16
MORE SCHOOL

As I entered my senior year at Prairie, I assumed that during this final year I would find a compatible mission agency and begin the application process. By the second semester, though, I began to think that maybe God wanted me to get further college training. The thought was not appealing. I had worked hard at Prairie and was tired—ready to be finished with school. I told the Lord so.

"I am tired of school. I don't want to do any more. Unless you put me in a corner where it is very clear that is what you want, I will not go on."

Hoping that no such corner would appear, I obtained a preliminary application form from a mission agency that seemed like a good fit for me. Aimed at a brief introduction, the application didn't ask for many details. I said I wanted to work with a tribe somewhere. I also felt it only fair that I mention my general physical limitations. I was confident they wouldn't be a negative factor because I had always been able to get around, under or over my body's limits in some way and do what I wanted to do. With just a couple weeks of school left, I mailed the application.

OK, after graduation I'll go home, relax a couple of weeks, and then take the next steps this agency requires.

My confidence soared as I went through the whole April 1969 graduation ceremony, even walking down the long aisle and up onto the stage without my crutches.

My parents and my brother Dick had come to my graduation. As we drove home, my happy optimism rode along with us. Once home, I waited for the reply to come from the mission agency.

In two weeks, it came. "We are sorry," it read, "but it has been our experience that people with less severe handicaps than yours can't make it on the foreign mission field. We suggest that you find a ministry in North America where you can serve the Lord."

Shock. Bone-rattling.

I went over the letter again. Never before had my physical limitations (I refused to think of myself as disabled) been a brick wall, blocking me from something I wanted to do. How could I even admit that it had happened? I agreed with the writer of that letter that many places in North America needed God's workers. But I also knew that wasn't what God had for me.

Through my tears, I remembered the bargain I had made with the Lord. There was only one thing to do—enroll in Whitworth in Spokane.

I determined I was not going to saddle myself with debt but also not ask my parents to finance my getting a degree from another school. Though Prairie Bible Institute wasn't an accredited school at the time, Whitworth accepted a year's worth of credits from PBI. I filled out Whitworth's application and financial aid application forms.

I soon became a student with a scholarship that covered most of my tuition and a grant that included the rest. I chose speech and drama (language arts) as my major. My minors were in education and journalism. Why these choices? Because they sounded enjoyable. I did not realize that I would use all these communication skills in my work for the rest of my life. Now I often counsel young people, "God knows how he made you. Make school and work choices based on what sounds enjoyable, and you're almost sure to get it right."

Wanting to get through Whitworth as soon as possible, after the regular school year I enrolled in a summer class too. And so began my year-round march of classes.

Whitworth was just twenty minutes from my parents' home, so I stayed at home rather than in a dorm. My dad bought me a new Datsun and found someone who would custom design and install driving controls for me. The next step was to learn how to drive. I got a permit, and my friend Cheri (who would later become my sister-in-law) served as my driving instructor—with lots of laughs. My brothers did not think it at all funny, though, when I got my license in only two weeks, a record for our family. Cheri and I began to carpool to school.

Someone suggested to me that the state Vocational Rehab might pay for my gas and textbooks. I should apply.

"No! I don't need any rehabilitation. I can already do everything I need to. I'm not being rehabilitated!"

"Elinor, think. This is what your dad has paid his taxes for all these years. It's owed to him and you. Just apply and see what happens."

I did. Besides filling out papers, this meant going in person to the Vocational Rehab office and talking with a representative. He was a kind man and seemed genuinely pleased to approve my getting help.

In this way, all my expenses were covered. I even had a bit of gas money left over at the end of each month. There was no doubt that God was directing it all. It was my job to study as hard as I could to keep the scholarship and learn everything I could.

The summer before my last semester at Whitworth, I felt God once again prodding me to investigate mission agencies.

"Father," I prayed, "You know I'm scared that I will be turned down again. If my being a missionary is truly your idea as I believe it is, please make it happen."

I wrote to Mr. Douglas at PBI asking if he could suggest some mission agencies that work among tribal people. He sent me the names and addresses of three agencies. When I wrote to them, I explained my physical limitations as I had done for that one agency before. I thought, *The one that is the Lord's choice will say I may apply.*

The other two will reject me, not thinking I'm strong enough. Instead, all three invited me to apply. Oh! Now what do I do? The only thing to do was ask the Lord what his choice was.

I was learning a lot about the ways God guides.

It wasn't long before there was a quiet assurance in my heart that I should apply to Regions Beyond Missionary Union (RBMU).

During this process, I confided to Cheri, "I will graduate soon, and I'm tired of school. I don't want to do more, but I am afraid that God wants me to take more classes."

I was right. When I applied to RBMU, they not only invited me to the August candidate school but also requested that I attend the Summer Institute of Linguistics (SIL) at the University of Oklahoma during the early summer months. All I knew about linguistics was that it is about languages. I assumed it would help me to learn the language wherever I ended up, but I had no idea about its complexities.

I graduated from Whitworth in February 1972, so I had a few months to rest before school began at SIL. It was the first break I'd had from school for almost three years. Besides rest from studying, it also gave me time to earn some cash selling jewelry at house parties before I drove from home to SIL in Norman, Oklahoma. Along the way, I stopped in Boise to see my sister and in Colorado to visit a friend.

This was before the era of cell phones and wide-spread credit card use. My dad made sure my car was in good shape and showed me how to diagnose and make simple repairs. I went to my bank, took out a big wad of cash, and began my journey.

Only now do I understand the courage it took for my parents to show not one indication of fear as I set out on what would ultimately be a complete solo cross-country trip. From Oklahoma, I would drive to RBMU candidate school in Philadelphia, Pennsylvania, then across the continent again back to Washington State. To me, it was a great adventure. To them, it was a brave launching of their daughter into the Lord's hands, just as they had done in the early days of my polio.

That summer of concentrated, accelerated linguistics classes was the toughest studying I had done yet. But my grades showed I did well and loved it. To me it was a game, in phonetics class, when we had to mimic a whole string of unknown language as it was spoken just to get used to that. It was fun to learn that the human mouth, tongue, and throat are instruments that can make more sounds than I ever imagined, and it was fun to make those sounds and learn how to write them down.

Learning how to do the sentence-level analysis of an unwritten language was fun, too, but analyzing discourse beyond sentence level nearly fried my brain.

The University of Oklahoma was a pedestrian-only campus, with sometimes long distances between buildings. I was not using crutches by then and often had to stop and rest on the way to class. My roommate was determined that by the end of summer, I would have gained enough strength to run. I didn't, but I did enjoy the good-natured challenge.

Another challenge was the stairway in the dorm. When I applied to SIL, I had not mentioned that I was disabled. They put me on the top floor, the fourth floor of the dorm, and there was no elevator. Sometimes when a group of us arrived back from class at the same time, one of the guys would put me on his back, and we would race everyone to the top floor. The laugh relieved our brain-stress.

RBMU sent most candidates or appointee missionaries to SIL for the sake of learning how to learn a language. When I finished SIL with the grades I had, the possibility of language analysis and writing an unwritten language plus Bible translation were among the arsenal of skills I could now offer to a mission field.

RBMU had asked if I were accepted, would I prefer going to Peru; Kalimantan, Indonesia; or Irian Jaya (now Papua), Indonesia. I knew it was either Peru or Irian Jaya. Kalimantan didn't sound right to me. I kept waiting for that quiet assurance in my heart about Peru or Irian Jaya, but it didn't come. I couldn't pick. One day I thought it was one place, the next day, the other choice.

At SIL I met a married couple who were also going to RBMU candidate school afterward. Dave and Kathy Tucker had already chosen Irian Jaya. So had a single guy, Johnny, who had just joined Unevangelized Fields Mission (UFM). This interest gave the four of us somewhat of a bond. As the end of SIL drew near, we talked about our travel plans from there. Johnny needed to get to Nashville and did not have a car. We planned that Johnny would ride with me as far as Nashville, Tennessee. The Tuckers and I would meet at a motel in Nashville and drive in tandem from there to Philadelphia. I managed to keep the Tuckers in sight as I followed them to and into Philadelphia, a city confusingly huge to me.

Whew! I would have been lost by now for sure! I thought as we pulled up to the old stone duplex which housed the RBMU office and guest quarters. Ancient oaks shaded that quiet old city street. In my mind, I could see the horses and wagons that used to trot under those trees. But a tinge of anxiety dampened my relief and intrigue.

Will I be accepted into the mission after these two weeks of candidate school? Will I go home to try again with another agency, or to get ready for . . . where?

I still could not decide between Peru and Irian Jaya.

Chapter 17

"IN" OR "OUT"?

After introductions and instructions, someone showed us where we single gals would stay during our time at candidate school. It was an outbuilding remade from the original horse carriage house into a type of bunkhouse. I was right—this neighborhood had been made for the days of horse and buggy. Fun!

The mission hostess who lived in an apartment in the duplex was the glue that held things together during the two weeks of candidate school. Bertel Vine, a very proper British lady, had been a Regions Beyond Missionary Union missionary in India before coming to the US to help her father, Ebenezer Vine, establish an American branch of RBMU. She coiled her graying hair in a roll behind her head from ear to ear. Miss Vine's dresses were somehow both utilitarian and stylishly modest. Miss Vine and volunteers or candidate helpers prepared all our meals, and she presided over mealtimes. Her sweet countenance made strict adherence to proper etiquette (or learning the rules of etiquette, for those unschooled in it) a pleasure—almost a game, waiting to see who would slip up. Miss Vine always gently corrected a mistake, saying that we needed to know how to conduct ourselves with respect in other peoples' homes. We even learned the proper way to open a soft-boiled egg. Miss Vine took her role as our teacher of civility seriously but lovingly.

Miss Vine also assigned us household chores. The point of these, I learned later, was to see how we worked with others, how we took orders, and how thorough and diligent we were at a task.

My job was to vacuum the basement every other day. Handling an upright vacuum was more of a challenge for me than the canister type I was used to, but I managed with only a few furniture bumps and scrapes. Miss Vine kindly never mentioned those blunders. Bless her!

Besides our daily devotional times together, we candidates also had classes that covered the history of RBMU, current policies and practices, an introduction to each of the geographical areas where RBMU worked, the mission's doctrinal parameters, and the like. We also took psychological and personality tests.

They also assigned each of us to a small team for local ministry. I was in the group that went to a rescue mission and held a pre-meal preaching and singing service. Going to a rescue mission was another new experience for me. Located in a building that looked like it was built in the 1800s, the structure had not changed much since then. We sat with the audience of men on unpadded wooden pews in the dark, stark, depressing sanctuary. The odor of the air was a combination of old wood, old clothes, and unwashed bodies. I knew pity was not appropriate but was unsure how I ought to feel. Mainly I wondered if any of them were at a stage to turn to God and sincerely prayed some were.

A fun weekend break between the two weeks of seriousness was the Saturday outing planned for us. We got on a local commuter train and went sight-seeing. I can still see the Liberty Bell as it was that day. For me, it was also a cross-cultural experience. We only have city buses in the northeast corner of Washington State.

Through the whole two weeks, my mind still went back and forth between the choice of Peru or Irian Jaya, but the more pressing question was whether they would accept me to work under RBMU at all. The final event of candidate school was a private interview with the RBMU board. At least half of the group were gray haired. They all sat in a solemn circle. There was one empty chair where I would sit. I don't remember the first few questions. I suppose they were supposed to help set me at ease. They didn't. Then came the clincher.

"You do realize, don't you, that due to your physical condition, we may decide that we don't want to risk sending you to one of our fields, all of which are physically rugged?"

"Yes," I said, though inside I said *No*.

"How would you react if that were the case?"

"It would throw me for a loop for a short while. That is what happened when an agency rejected me a few years back. But I recovered, and I do know one thing: If you don't accept me, somebody will, because I know for sure that God wants me to do tribal work."

How did that come out of my mouth? It was entirely out of character with all the training I had received about being respectful to one's elders. At age twenty-five, I was not nearly as assertive as I grew to be in later years. I was half embarrassed but half not, knowing it was the truth. With that, the questions were over. The board prayed aloud for me and their decision, and I was free to go.

Then I waited. Each of the candidates was privately called to someone's office and told the news. The board assigned Miss Vine to do that for me. She gently told me, "The board could not decide about you. Usually, if the vote is not unanimous, we mark it as a no. On the other hand, maybe even just one person with the opposite decision is right. In your case, the board did not want to take a lack of unanimity as no. They want to be confident their choice is correct. They agreed that each would pray about it daily for a week without consulting each other and come back next Saturday to make the final decision. Would it be possible for you to stay for another week?"

It was possible—I had no plans except for driving back across the continent to home whenever that worked out. I had no deadlines.

"Yes, I can stay."

"Good. We will close up the carriage house, but there is a bedroom upstairs where you can stay, and you may eat meals with me."

I knew how special this all was when I discovered that two other candidates had been rejected. The mission was doing something unusual in my case.

In my heart, I knew that RBMU was God's choice. But I still didn't know if God wanted me in Peru or Irian Jaya. I had a whole blank week ahead of me to find out. "Blank" in the sense that the program was over. My time was mine to use as I wanted.

Lord, please show me for certain where you want me to go.

I spent a lot of time praying and a lot of time memorizing the first two chapters of Hebrews—something I had wanted to do for some time. I did little things to help Miss Vine, too, but spent most of my time memorizing and praying. Before the end of the week, I knew that Irian Jaya was God's choice. No bolt from the blue told me—I just knew.

On Saturday morning, I helped Miss Vine prepare snacks and set a proper table of refreshments for the special meeting of the RBMU board. As I did, my heart beat a bit fast and my palms were sweaty. Each board member smiled and greeted me as they arrived, but still, I was nervous. They went into the boardroom. Miss Vine and I waited. More quickly than I expected, the meeting was over. When they came out of the room, a spokesman said, "We all came here today knowing that you are to be accepted to serve with RBMU and go to Irian Jaya."

Wow, what a confirmation that I was on the right track. That affirmation was to serve me well in future difficult times in Irian Jaya.

Chapter 18

SOLO CROSS-CONTINENT DRIVE

With the RBMU board's decision behind me, over the weekend I got ready for the long drive home. I knew I would probably never have the chance for a cross-country trip by car again, so I mapped out a plan that would hit all the appealing places I reasonably could along the way.

After I successfully negotiated not getting lost leaving Philadelphia, I drove to a Pennsylvania Dutch Amish area where I found a farm that conducted tours. What a fun beginning to my trip.

From there I drove north, hoping to find a hotel near Niagara Falls. I did, and the next morning, I saw the falls from both the Canadian and American sides. From there I headed west.

As I traveled, I chose as many alternate routes as I could so I could see "real" things, not just superhighway byways. I avoided big cities. Whenever I came upon a historic landmark sign, I pulled off to see it, taking as much time as I wanted. I had no definite schedule except to get home before my cash ran out.

As I drove through the countrysides, I looked for fruit stands. It was end-of-summer harvest time. Apples, pears, and peaches were tasty portable food. When I added a yogurt cup from a grocery store, it was a cheaper meal than I could get at a restaurant or café. Sometimes, though, I got a drive-in hamburger or even—as a treat—stopped at a diner.

I would have loved to tell my parents each night what I saw that day, but long-distance calls from phone booths were expensive. I usually just sent postcards to Mom and Dad along the way, telling them where I was so they could follow my progress. Each day I drove until the sun began to get low in the sky, then looked for a motel. Keeping safety in mind (though it wasn't the problem it would be today for a single young woman traveling alone) and wanting to save what money I could, I looked for a moderately priced, reasonably maintained motel each time. Only one night the whole trip did I not find a motel and had to sleep in my car under a light at a rest stop.

I saw a famous cave or two, maybe Mammoth or Carlsbad or both—I can't remember. I drove by endless miles of Iowa cornfields, a real preserved sod house on the Midwest prairies, monuments like Mount Rushmore, and geographical features like the Badlands. I had so much fun exploring what sounded interesting during the day and stopping for the night wherever I was. After an intense summer of linguistics study and candidate school, the trip was the relaxation I needed for body, mind, and spirit. I had a lot to think through and plan how I would approach finding financial sponsors for my missionary career. RBMU was not well-known in the West. I could do my thinking and praying in an unhurried manner.

The last day, though, I was under a crunch. I had spent most of my remaining cash at a hotel near Yellowstone National Park. I didn't have enough for another night. I had to make that long drive through Montana, across the Idaho panhandle, and to Spokane before gas and hamburger money ran out. I made it home at twilight, just before sunset. I had only $1.25 left in my pockets.

The past years had been a season of intellectual, spiritual, and physical challenges. My confidence in God was stronger than ever. No longer the cocky world-by-the tail eighteen-year-old, I was a young woman in her mid-twenties who had matured a lot, and though I had much more to go, I was ready to tackle the challenges of finding supporters, gathering supplies I would need for my first term, getting a passport and visa, and getting to Irian Jaya.

Chapter 19

BUILDING MY TEAM

It was time to find people who would pray for me and financially support me and the needs of my work in Irian Jaya. During my growing-up years, I had seen my parents' joy and commitment to giving to missionaries. In more recent years, I had observed the stress and exhaustion of many missionaries who were on furlough from where they worked, traveling to all corners of the continental United States as they visited supporting friends and churches. Surely there was a better way!

Lord, on my home leaves, I want to be in my church much of the time, letting the people get reacquainted with me enough to see me as a person just like them, except working for you faraway in a different culture and language. But not doing that inside some superior bubble of holiness not available to them. I don't want to be away, traveling all the time. So would you please show me enough people and churches in northern Idaho, Washington, and northern Oregon to cover what I need in prayer and money?

I also honestly wanted to take the joy of talking about God's love for the whole world into small rural churches who rarely had a visiting missionary. I'm ashamed to say that many fellow missionaries did not contact small churches or turned down invitations from them because that's not where the money is. Shame on us! I don't know if that Chinese man who spoke to the handful of Chattaroy area farm families many years ago got any money that night. But God used him to make firm a commitment to missions in the life of one young girl. How much money is that worth?

In the West, RBMU was known in only a few places in California. Headquarters in Philadelphia had given me the phone numbers or addresses of a few people in my region who had contributed to the mission once or twice. "Few" being a handful. Not only was I an unknown to the pastors I would try to contact, so was my mission organization. Besides that, I wanted to go to small, rural churches, not large, city churches. Support raising could take a while!

This was long before the internet existed. I began with a phone book that included rural areas in my own and adjoining counties. I looked up small churches in outlying areas and phoned.

"Hello. My name is Elinor Young. Regions Beyond Missionary Union just accepted me to go to Irian Jaya, Indonesia, as a missionary. I would love to come to your church to encourage your people with a report about what God is doing around the world."

"Well, but we don't have any money to give you."

"That's OK. Money is not my aim. I will come for nothing. I just want to encourage your people. I attend a small church and know how seldom we get missionary speakers, compared to larger churches."

One, then two agreed and scheduled a Sunday. Those pastors took more of a risk than I did. They had no idea whether this woman could deliver on her promise. I hadn't even been a missionary yet and might be a dry, bumbling speaker. But I knew God could encourage hearts to give, even if a church couldn't. The few churches who let me come would have pastor friends' contact information they might give me. Sure enough, bit by bit, the connections and invitations grew. So did promises of financial support.

RBMU also requested I gather and pack into shipping crates or fifty-gallon drums all the household items I would need in Irian Jaya. The Irian Jaya field sent me a list of things from a mouli food grinder, to cotton dresses, to a hammer and saw. Pages of things I couldn't buy there. My parents' house had nowhere to store all those things nor a basement in which to build crates. My dad recruited the basement of a friend, and some men from our church built them.

In less than a year, I had gathered all my financial support and equipment so I could apply for my visa. RBMU asked that I travel to Irian Jaya with the Donaldson family, also new missionaries from Washington State. We would leave from Los Angeles, California, on December 7, 1973.

Chapter 20

NOT THE NANNY

My flight would leave Spokane in the afternoon. That was good because I still had last-minute shopping and packing to do that morning. Dad helped me, and we barely finished in time to leave for the airport.

Mom, Dad, and I had a cup of coffee in the terminal before my flight. Then it came—the announcement to board.

As I walked out to the plane and up the steps, I could see Dad in his green sweater, standing at the window watching. I still clearly saw Dad as I gave one last wave before I stepped into the plane.

I was a novice at airplane travel. I had flown to just two places and back. At those times, all I had to do was show up.

This trip was different. I had a layover in Los Angeles. The airport there was confusingly huge, and I was alone. I was supposed to gather my luggage and get to Korean Airlines, then they would tell me where they had reserved a room for the night and how to get there. I had no idea how to do all that.

When I entered the LAX terminal, I saw a sign pointing to the baggage pickup area. I took a deep breath, prayed a quick "help," and stepped out.

I found the baggage area. All good so far.

By the time my luggage came down the chute, nearly all the other passengers were gone. I had no trouble getting a porter. I told him my situation—I needed to go to Korean Airlines to check about my hotel reservation. The porter took me to the bus stop and told me to get on the bus and stay until it got me there. Korean Airlines was in a different building from United.

One of the men standing at the bus stop must have heard me asking the porter how much the bus fare was, and he must have seen how new I was at all this. He helped me put my luggage on the bus and watched it for me. He also helped me take it off. Maybe I just looked helpless!

After my next porter took me and my luggage to the Korean Airlines desk and then out to wait for the hotel limousine, I asked him if I owed him anything, and how much. His face registered half embarrassment and half disbelief as he said, "Yes, it's courtesy. One dollar is normal." I smiled, said, "OK," and gave him a dollar and my thanks.

And so I began learning how to be a world traveler.

That night the phone in my hotel room rang. It was from Miss Vine. "God bless you, dear, as you set out in the morning. Let me pray for you." Now I felt truly ready for the adventure.

Don Richter, the RBMU representative who lived in Los Angeles and who would help me and the Donaldson family get on the first leg of our overseas flight, also phoned me that night. He asked if I could manage to take a cab to the airport in the morning. The Donaldsons would fill his car, with no room for me. If I couldn't get a cab, he would drop them off and get me. By now I knew how to get a cab at least, so that was no issue. That last-minute call should have clued me in to another problem—one I would discover in the morning.

I met everyone at the airport the next morning. There were Dr. and Marge Donaldson and five young children, from their twelve-year-old daughter to two-year-old Philip dragging his blankie and stick horsey. His four sisters had all sorts of stuff, much of it not in bags. Everyone had their bits and pieces. The closest to what might be called a carry-on bag was the Barbie doll and clothes in a doll-size Barbie suitcase. *Why didn't they put some of this in luggage and check it through?* Because their checked bags were already over the weight limit. Oh my, this was going to be quite a trip.

Our first overnight destination was Seoul, South Korea, but we made two stops on the way. The first was Honolulu, then Tokyo. Both times it took a while to get five kids moving in the right direction and assign each of them part of the kit and caboodle. I noticed that airline personnel, guides, and fellow passengers regarded us with pained, impatient expressions. I could also tell that they thought I was the nanny. I smiled to myself and thought, *You're not far wrong.*

Next was Seoul, then Hong Kong and on to Singapore. The airlines paid for our overnight hotels in each place.

At Hong Kong, they said, "There is a problem with your ticket. It must be re-written, but no desks are open now. You'll have to do it in the morning."

The next morning, they sent me in circles from one airline to another and back again. Finally, at bundle-of-nerves stage, I found someone at the Cathay Airlines counter who was willing to do more than shove me off on someone else. While she was calling around for me, I asked, "Is there any chance of my making this flight to Jakarta, Indonesia?"

"No," she replied, and the pressure lifted. No more nerves.

Calmed down now, I was able to continue rationally. The Cathay Pacific passenger service agent told me that she would call Singapore Airlines—they would take care of me. "Go back there." I did, and sure enough, one of the agents was on the phone. A brand-new face popped on the scene, all smiles. I don't know where he came from, but his face was a welcome one.

"You missed this flight, but we will get you on a later flight. OK?"

I smiled back. "Yes, that will be fine. But will you please wire Mr. Donaldson at our guest house in Jakarta and tell him which flight I will arrive on?"

One of the men at the desk left, and in a few minutes came back with a new ticket.

Why did they not do that before?

Another agent helped me take my luggage to the storage area.

When it was time to check in for my flight to Jakarta, I discovered that Garuda Airlines would not waive extra baggage fees as other airlines had done. I didn't have much cash and decided to check just my suitcase and carry my other, smaller bag.

At twenty-five pounds, that bag got mighty heavy as I tramped around the Singapore terminal looking for the Garuda gate. As I write this, there is no way I could lift twenty-five pounds, and even at the time, carrying it slowed me down and wore me out, but in the end, I was glad I had that bag.

"We didn't have time to transfer your checked suitcase to this plane. Are you willing to travel without it?" All I cared about was getting to Jakarta, so I said yes.

Chapter 21

FIRST INTRODUCTION TO INDONESIA

When I landed at Jakarta, someone handed me a message that said my suitcase would come at 8:30 the next morning. Missionaries from the Inter-Mission Business Office (IMBO) guest house picked me up, and I enjoyed some sleep.

The next morning, the Donaldsons and I left the IMBO guest house for the airport at 4:30 a.m. Once there, we met even more mass confusion than at other airports. We certainly needed the Indonesian help supplied by our IMBO hosts. The IMBO guy told me, "Your flight leaves before the one comes that has your other bag. I'll send it to Sentani, Irian Jaya, with some people who will pass through Saturday." Until then, all I had for clothes was what I carried.

I'm so glad I didn't check that bag!

Our flight's departure was delayed. By 6:00 a.m., it was uncomfortably stuffy inside the terminal, so we went outside to wait.

Are we being gawked at because we are white or because of the pile of luggage where we are perched?

Finally, we boarded the plane, and I wished for the outside air. The airplane stunk as if any cleaning was a long time ago, and there was no air conditioning while we sat on the tarmac.

Our destination was Biak, just north of the big island of Irian Jaya, Indonesia, and its neighbor, the nation of Papua New Guinea. We would spend the night in Biak. We landed at Biak at 4:00 p.m., four international times zones east of Jakarta. We were glad to finish flying for the day and to be out of big city life.

Tropical birds and insects began their evening concert as we walked from the tiny Biak airport to our hotel. Small children gaped at the cart piled with our luggage and stared at Philip's horsey, our white skins, and our Western clothes. As soon as we put our things in our rooms, we went outside to do our own gazing at the unfamiliar scene.

The ocean bay sang its splash-song not far from the courtyard and palm-lined beach our rooms faced. The song was as strong from inside our rooms as it was outside, thanks to glassless screened windows and doors. The breeze that came through made the hot, humid air somewhat tolerable. The floors of our rooms were solid, but the hallway floors were slats placed an inch apart. Since the building was on stilts, those gaps not only let air flow up and in but also let broom sweepings drop through.

On the way to the dining room for supper, we stopped to look at a big parrot chained to a perch and at some other birds in cages, all just outside the kitchen. Beth Donaldson spotted more wildlife in the dining room: lizards on the walls and ceiling. It was our first encounter with the ever-present geckos of the jungle areas.

During supper, the lights went off and back on a few times, apparently to change or re-fuel generators. The rice, fish soup, and vegetables we had were delicious. The Donaldson girls, though, ate almost nothing. They didn't like any of it.

Maybe the changes have been too quick for them, and who can blame them? But they'll get hungry if they don't adapt soon. I hoped they would.

The next cultural surprise was hard not just for the girls but also for me to accept. A sheet covered each bed, and when we pulled each one back, there was only a bare mattress underneath.

I guess we're supposed to sleep on top of this one sheet. The dirty blanket on the end of the bed must be to cover us if we get chilly. I hope I don't.

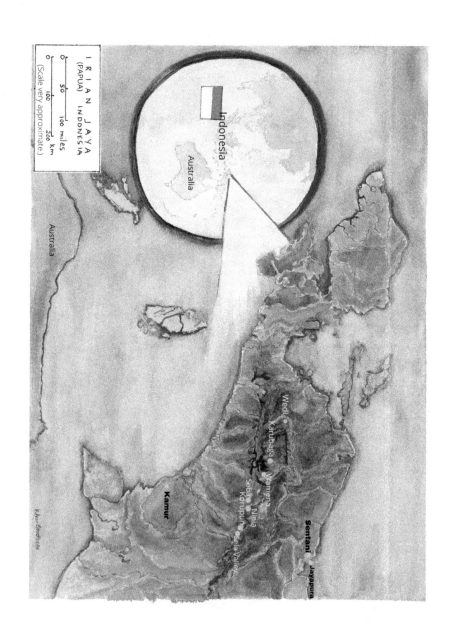

IRIAN JAYA
(PAPUA) INDONESIA

0   50   100 miles
0   100   200 km
(Scale very approximate)

Indonesia

Australia

Australia

Wedi
Katubaga
Wamena
Soba Nipia
Korupun Sela Valley
Kamur
Sentani Jayapura

Chapter 22

IRIAN JAYA AT LAST

Just after noon the next day, we left Biak on the smallest plane yet—it had just nine rows of seats. We entered at the back and walked uphill to our spots.

Does it need to be pointed up to give it a head start taking off?

The lumbering flight to the main island took two hours. That small plane couldn't fly high, and I loved the close view of Irian Jaya—the big, winding, dust-colored rivers pouring into the sea, and range upon range of mountains. The closer ones were deep green; the further ones blue, and finally faint blue. White fluffy clouds floated in the rich blue sky.

We landed at Jayapura airport, located at Sentani, an hour inland from Jayapura. Missionaries from Sentani picked us up. I was to stay with the Rosenberger family until my flight to the interior in two or three weeks.

The first few days I went nowhere. I was exhausted from the long trip and after that was sick with something I picked up in Jakarta. When I recovered, I began to take in my surroundings.

The town of Sentani was just below a hill called Pos Tujuh where we stayed. The one main street was lined with stores, "tokos," that seemed packed with everything from food to machetes. A few tokos specialized in one or two products, but most carried a variety of goods. They sold luggage, bike seats, pen fillers, men's hats, hairspray, candy, yard goods, canned food, cassette tapes, and more. The tokos seemed to be very much alike, yet each supported a family. Sandwiched between a couple of these tokos was an open tailor shop with two treadle machines. I peeked in and saw a man behind one of those and another man doing hand work in light so dim I didn't know how he could see. Some van-like vehicles used as taxis hurried along that street with what seemed like hundreds of motorbikes and motor scooters. Here and there a dog yapped from an unknown location. Vehicles and bikes drove with their horns as much as with accelerators. People spoke loudly above the noise. To me, their speech sounded like run-on babble.

The odor of vehicle and motorbike exhaust combined with the smell of the re-used oil that was cooking fried food along the sidewalks. The stink of animal dung along the way also hit my nose. All those mixed with ever-present clove-laced cigarette smoke to create an unwelcome, alien waft.

Sights, sounds, and odors combined into one voice that said I was, indeed, a foreigner.

Getting documents filled out and signed came first after the days we rested. Field Director Dave Martin took us to Jayapura to do that. Dave's wife, Margy, went along. "I need to get some new sandals," she said.

Oh, so we'll see a shoe shop?

Not far down the road, my eyes popped, and I grabbed whatever was closest in the van-like vehicle as we took tight blind corners while on-coming drivers ignored that we belonged on "our" side of the road and they on theirs. We also dodged potholes, people, goats, and domestic banteng (Bali cattle).

In later years, I came to realize that this first ride to Jayapura was a "soft landing" introduction. It was in a mission-owned vehicle with a missionary driver. I was to travel that road many, many times the more local way. A letter to a friend explained that mode of travel:

Privately owned vehicles are few; the backbone of
public transportation are the taxis, which are nine-
passenger (counting the driver) mini-buses. The road
between Sentani and Jayapura winds and writhes
like a snake in pain for the whole hour's journey. The

drivers can't stand to have anyone in front of them, and blind curves (which they all are) are no deterrent to their incessant passing. Likewise, speeding taxis are no deterrent to the people, goats, cows, dogs, and anything else that figures it has as much right to the road as motorized objects. And there are no shoulders on roads. At night people lie crosswise on the pavement, with their heads toward the center, soaking up its lingering warmth and chatting with their buddies. If you hit anyone lying or walking on the road, it is your fault. No matter what.

I continued in that later letter,

Not long ago, I had been working with my two language helpers in Abepura, halfway between Jayapura and Sentani. At the end of the day, we were on our way back to where we were staying in Sentani. It is not unusual for taxis to squeeze in several passengers over the limit, but I looked very dubiously at the one that stopped to pick us up. I didn't think we could all get in, but the "conductor" (a young boy who sits on a stool by the side door and collects passengers and their fees), insisted there was room. By some people sitting on the edge of the seats and some sitting back, we all managed to find a spot. As we roared down the road, I took a headcount. Actually, "roared" is the wrong word. We were so overloaded the driver couldn't get up speed and was forced to take the curves slowly. There were thirteen of us—all adults. Besides that, the fellow next to me clutched a flour sack with a large bird called a hornbill in it. The head, with its three-inch-thick and six-inch-long curved beak, stuck out of the sack as it desperately flailed about in its struggle for freedom. Despite the crowded conditions, I kept my legs away!

That letter was some years after this first trip to Jayapura when I knew nothing of the coming adventures.

The seemingly countless tokos in Jayapura held an astounding variety of goods compared to Sentani, but Margy couldn't find any women's sandals that fit. She finally settled for some men's sandals.

That much walking made me tired, so I went to sit in our vehicle and people-watched.

I noticed three types of people in Irian Jaya. Indonesians from other islands have dark straight hair and light brown skin, like other Malay-related groups of Southeast Asia. There were also Chinese people. They seemed to be the wealthiest and were the businessmen. Finally, there were the Irianese/Papuans. Like other Melanesians, they have dark skin and dark kinky hair. Over the years, I learned the distinctive facial and structural features of different Papuan tribes.

I noticed that the clothing of all the people was very colorful, except for the poorest among them. The ethnic Indonesian men wore black caps and ankle-length wraparound skirts, though some of the younger ones wore Western, very stylish clothing—nice slacks with bright shirts. Sometimes bright pants too. The poorer people had baggier pants, more drab-colored shirts, and often no shoes.

The women's styles were more uniform than the men's. Western-style skirts and blouses or dresses were the norm. Occasionally, I saw a long Asian wraparound skirt. The fit, color, and cleanliness of a woman's clothes marked her class. Those with little money had very poorly fitted, dirty dresses with little or nothing underneath. Those who could afford new clothes bought them or had them made fitting about as tight as they dared.

I saw way more women than men carrying things. Men who did carry something usually didn't have a woman along to do it. Big loads were placed on the head and nearly always steadied by one hand.

Women carried babies in a broad, long piece of cloth draped over one shoulder and under the other arm, then tied. The baby rode inside, next to her mother's chest, where she would be if she were in her mother's arms. Because the cloth was so broad, it could expand as the baby grew. Carrying the baby this way left the mother's hands free to hold other things.

I talked with a missionary who carried her baby that way. She thought it was the best thing ever invented. She said that when her twin boys were babies, she carried them both that way—one on either side. She did that when she and her husband went back to North America for leave, and when she stepped off the plane, her mother about had fits. In the early 1970s, baby-carrying methods like this were not yet popular in the West.

As I people-watched that day, I also saw men carrying two items on either end of a long pole balanced on a shoulder. I didn't ever see women move things that way. One man had what looked like two large metal drums hanging from the ends of his pole. The drums looked incredibly heavy; I couldn't fathom why his shoulder didn't break.

And so through my eyes, nose, ears, and even mouth as I ate new kinds of food, I began to learn about this land that was to become my home.

Chapter 23
CULTURAL IMPRESSIONS

With the long, puzzling immigration process in Jayapura finished, the next step was to fly interior to a conference center where RBMU had an Indonesian language school for new missionaries from our mission agency and others. However, that flight wouldn't happen until after Christmas and the New Year.

During my trip to Jayapura for paperwork, I had met the single missionary women who lived in an apartment above the office of The Missions Fellowship (TMF). TMF served the missionaries of all evangelical mission agencies in Irian Jaya. They helped with our paperwork, filled orders of supplies, and got them to Mission Aviation Fellowship (MAF) in Sentani so they could be flown to our interior posts, and they served in other ways that helped us to live and work in Irian Jaya.

"The TMF Girls," as we called them, invited me to stay with them for a few weeks, including Christmas, while I waited to fly to Karubaga in the interior mountains for language school. I had been staying with the Rosenbergers on Pos Tujuh near Sentani. Now, though, I packed up my few things and went to be with The Girls in Jayapura.

Yes, "few things." I still had only the one bag I had carried onto the plane. Despite promises, my checked bag hadn't come. I had only two dresses and a few other things in the carry-on. I managed that way for three weeks. Welcome to missionary life.

That was a Christmas like no other. The first Christmas program I went to, put on by one of the Indonesian churches the

Town Girls attended, was two hours late—typically Indonesian. Even Indonesians joke about their "rubber time." I was surprised that the second program I went to—a kids' program—was just one hour late.

It began with a singing, marching parade of all the children. At least, that's what it was supposed to be. The leader ushered in all the preschoolers, each wearing a paper sheep's head and carrying a lit candle. They were supposed to march in front of the stage, stand in a line, and sing, "This Little Light of Mine." But it didn't turn out that way. They came in only as they were led or pushed by the lady in charge, some singing and some not. Here and there, one stopped to relight his candle with his friend's or went to join her chum at the beginning, end, or middle of the pack. I held my breath the whole time, sure that someone was going to catch on fire from handling the candles that way.

Then the leader went back into the wings to round up the older kids to join the lineup and song. Problem was, all the little kids followed her into the wings, so she had to again herd everybody back up there together.

Between performances, we sang a carol or two. We had song sheets, and because Indonesian is written consistently phonetically and I knew the tunes, I was able to sort of sing along, even though I didn't know the language.

Four girls came out on stage and sang a song, accompanying themselves with dance-like hand gestures while gracefully picking up and putting down their feet in a ballet-like march in place. One of the girls was exceptionally graceful—beautiful to watch. Edai, one of my new friends, explained, "She's Javanese."

One of the TMF Girls told me the story of the dance. "The song talks about a child in his mother's arms and how he is innocent, then grows and the burden of sin becomes heavy on his back. He will perish with it unless he turns to Jesus and confesses with his mouth."

I thought, *Now there is a Christmas message!*

Christmas was celebrated on the streets too. Besides programs like these, one informal way the Indonesians celebrated Christmas was the music the tokos (stores) played. Just a few songs played loudly and constantly. They frequently chose an instrumental version of "My Grandfather's Clock." I never did figure out its connection with Christmas.

Chapter 24

WHAT'S AHEAD?

On Friday, December 28, I went with friends to a beach called Base G, where General McArthur and his men landed their amphibian boats during WWII. There were no signs of that in 1973, though, and I was in a contemplative mood. I had my journal with me and wrote:

> I'm sitting on the beach writing this. Just a few feet and coming closer is the Pacific Ocean. Big waves come roaring in, each just a bit closer than the last as if it were stretching to touch and greet me. Many have welcomed me to this land. Why not, too, the ocean which cradles it?

> Though we are on the north coast, at this spot I am facing east. Across the restless expanse in front of me is a land much more familiar to me, where the people I know and love are, and where my language is the common tongue, not this unintelligible combination of sounds constantly bombarding me.

> Yet I feel peace and contentment here. My heart and soul are at rest with a quiet joy, because slightly to my right, across this little inlet, I see what I came here to see. I spot range after range of mountains stretching deep into the interior. Behind these ranges are mountains I cannot see. On those mountains and between them are people I have not seen, that no Westerner has ever seen. People who have never seen or experienced the power of this ocean. But

more importantly, people who have never seen or experienced the power of the ocean's Creator—a force that can set them free from their miserable bondage to Satan. I've come to tell them of the release available to them. And I'm glad.

Chapter 25

ANOTHER WORLD

Less than a week later, I got into a small plane and flew to the mountain valley of Karubaga, where I and other recently arrived missionaries would attend the new Indonesian language school. After close to an hour of flying over what looked like an endless flat, swampy jungle, mountains rose before us abruptly. Foothills were few. As we approached the valley and the airstrip of Karubaga, villages of round thatched-roof dwellings dotted the mountainsides. Ribbon-like trails joined them and the cleared garden areas surrounding them. These people were part of the Western Dani tribe.

What is life like down there?

My breath became fast and shallow, and my palms felt damp. No more imagining. This was real.

We signaled our intent to land by circling low over the landing strip of Karubaga. People on the airstrip scattered. The pilot swung the plane wide and lined up with the strip. He keyed his radio microphone: "Mike Papa Delta landing Karubaga," he announced.

The ground seemed to rise as our wheels touched down. The rattle-like sound and feel confirmed that we were way out of any city's reach. It was a gravel airstrip—no asphalt here. We taxied to the top, spun around to face down the runway, and cut the engine. The waiting women at the side of the airstrip wore skirts made from grassy reeds. Large loosely knit bags made from local fibers hung from a band at the opening down the women's backs.

As soon as the propeller stopped spinning, a local Dani man put some wooden blocks hard in front of the tires so the plane couldn't roll downhill. Then the pilot opened the doors.

Dani hands helped me down. I walked to the edge of the airstrip and stood by a small shed while people unloaded the plane. A fiber-like, musty odor floated by as a grass skirt or net bag passed. So did an earthy, sweaty body odor that was new to me. Countless men, women, and children milled around, all talking at once, it seemed. Would I ever be able to make sense of such strange sounds?

I knew that though we were at Karubaga to learn Indonesian, the local people were Danis, and few spoke much of that language. They spoke Western Dani. The Western Dani tribe is one of three hundred to four hundred tribes who each have their own language and who at the time I arrived in Irian Jaya spoke little to no Indonesian.

White faces said "Welcome" and introduced themselves in English—that was familiar and comforting. They had hired an eager crew of helpers from the Dani tribe to carry our bags and bundles to our living quarters. One of the missionaries asked me to point out my things, then, in that strange Dani language, he instructed a Dani man where to take it. One of the missionary women told me to follow her to my cabin.

I was to learn that both men and women of the Dani tribe were hard workers and always eager to earn money or goods they could not otherwise obtain. There were only villages and missionaries here no stores or other commerce. Years earlier, the Danis had dropped their suspicious views of these strange white people and were glad to profit from their presence.

The new Indonesian language school would use the conference facilities at Karubaga. There was a kitchen-dining hall building, small bunk cabins, and two bathroom-shower buildings: men's and women's. The walls of all these buildings were rough-hewn boards. All structures had tin roofs. The kitchen-dining room had louvered glass windows. The other buildings had opaque plastic "window-lite" in frames one could prop open for air circulation or close against the rain. Nothing fancy.

After a day of orientation and getting acquainted, we soon settled into a routine of classes, meals, and cooking.

During our morning classes, we sat on benches around one of the long tables in the dining room. We each had our "Learning to Speak Indonesian" books in front of us as the missionary teacher went over the vocabulary and explained the grammar of the day's lesson. During afternoon classes, the teacher drilled us on both use and understanding of what we had studied up to then. The teacher dismissed us at mid-afternoon, but we were expected to get the day's lesson well into our heads before the next morning. Indonesian is a relatively simple language. The sounds are familiar to English speakers and don't include complications like tone. It has straightforward, consistent, easy-to-learn grammar rules and a basic subject-verb-object sentence structure.

In the kitchen, local helpers, men from the Dani tribe, chopped, sliced, and cleaned, but we had to plan, supervise, and cook our meals. Because the Dani helpers knew some simple Indonesian vocabulary, kitchen duty was an opportunity for basic language practice.

One day I pointed at some meat we were cooking and said to the Dani helper, "Daging babu." His face registered amusement. I was trying to say, "Meat of pig" (Daging babi), but instead I said, "Meat of a maid."

Language school at an interior tribal location and under the instruction of experienced missionaries was a useful way to begin to learn our new way of life. As we learned Indonesian in our classes, we also had many opportunities to walk through the local villages and gardens and to visit with the local missionaries and learn from them general skills we could apply to life in any isolated place.

At the six-week mark of the language course, our teacher gave us a four-day weekend break. Catching the festive spirit, everyone, including resident missionaries, decided that we should go on a picnic. So off we went. We hired a group of Dani men to carry our food and other picnic essentials. There were about fifty of us. The picnic spot was an hour's hike away over mountain footpaths that were more like goat paths—steep, narrow, and winding.

The first part of the path was easy. It started down toward the river, and gravity is always a great help when descending. Then it started to ascend nearly straight up and finally settled to a graded climb along the mountainside.

I started in great form. Over the weeks of walking around Karubaga, I had worked up a pace rapid enough to keep up with everyone else, except going uphill. And I had discovered how to go downhill without just creeping along.

But I couldn't keep up for an hour, especially at a climb. Three Dani men had me as their special assignment. One of them was Titur, a stocky little man not much taller than I was, who carried some of the supplies when not helping me. I was determined to go as far as I could by myself, and at first, the downhill part was doable. However, before long the trail became so steep I had to hang on to a guy on each side to keep my balance. They also had to help me over the bridge that was partway over the river, but when it came to the wading part, they insisted that I ride. Yes, ride—on someone's shoulders. The water was only ankle deep, but my helpers wouldn't go on otherwise, so up I went.

When you ride on a Dani man's shoulders, you don't go piggy-back. Your legs straddle his neck, and you hang on to his hair to keep your balance. Really! Then he takes off, and you grip. They carry their sick or injured friends that way. How someone sick or injured can hang on, I'm not sure.

Titur was the first to carry me. His shoulders were so narrow that I felt like I would fall off if I just grasped his hair, so I locked my hands under his chin. Poor guy!

When Titur got tired, Tom, another one of our carriers, took over. He was taller and had huge calves and thighs. These guys have powerful shoulders because that's where they carry everything from logs and bundles of firewood to injured friends. Tom took me up that extra steep part of the trail, and before we reached the top,

I was sure I was going to fall off. I couldn't seem to get my balance right. Since my spine is rigid from the fusions, I couldn't curl around Titur's or Tom's heads to keep a proper center of gravity. I had to lean forward, which pushed the poor guy's head forward. My thighs also got very tired trying to keep me perched up there.

Once Titur, Tom, and another helper, Teban, started to carry me, they seldom let me walk. They were proud of their responsibility and determined to do it well. The only time they let me down was when we came to the stiles in the pig fences. These stiles didn't look much different to me from other parts of the boundary fences except that they were where path intercepted fence. Usually, rocks or sticks were up against each side of these barricades, to act as a sort of step. You just had to climb over. Once, when Titur was carrying me, we approached a fence. I expected he would let me down and help me over, but no. He just climbed over with me on his shoulders.

That was one of the many times I noticed the way the Dani people use their feet. We Westerners have handicapped ourselves by wearing shoes. When Teban was carrying me, he came to a stile with only a three-inch branch fastened against the fence to act as a step. He wrapped his toes around that, and up and over we went. Going uphill and downhill in the mud where I could see no foothold at all, just a big toe would find something firm, and we would balance on it. Often the path was a mere couple of inches from a steep precipice, but their feet never missed solidly planting in the exact spot they needed to be.

It didn't take me long to feel safe perched on their shoulders, even though not comfortable.

Soon my carriers and I reached the front of the string of trekkers. We pulled way ahead going through the fields and villages. The only village inhabitants I saw were chickens and dogs. The people were in their mountainside gardens working or gathering food. Sometimes they hollered down at us in Dani something I assumed meant "Who do you have there?" because my carriers would answer, "Nona Elinod." (Miss Elinor—they don't have an English "r" sound.)

The people around us were gathering their day's needs as my ancestors had in another era. My Western world had become filled with the kind of strife the Danis had no knowledge of yet. With the sunshine warm and the air clean and pure, the mountains seemed to form a sheltering cradle. I felt a refreshing peace and calm. A release from the stifling pressure of the world at large. Not that I didn't realize that these people had their problems too. They did. But for the time being, they were not caught up in the turmoil, pressure, and problems of the rest of the world.

My helpers and I arrived at the picnic site about a half-hour before the last of our group. The spot was under tall trees on a steep, muddy incline on the other side of the river. This time, Tom was carrying me when we went five feet straight down to the river and waded across. Where Tom put his feet, I couldn't tell.

We sat on leaf-covered logs and ate our sandwiches, bananas, and oranges. The warm breeze rustled through the leaves of the trees and the tall grass. The blue sky held only a few white clouds. The river's splash was not so loud we couldn't hear each other talk. After a bit, we started back again. My carriers and I were the last to leave because I delayed leaving to take pictures. Nothing, though, could adequately capture the experience.

Chapter 26

ADJUSTMENTS

"The Commander airplane won't be coming. MAF has suspended our normally scheduled weekly flights while the fuel shortage lasts."

Oh, no! I thought. *What about the mail?*

The Commander was the larger single-engine airplane that brought in the big loads of supplies the missionaries and language school at Karubaga needed. Of even higher emotional priority was the mail it brought in and carried out. Letters were the only communication we had with the outside world once a week. But missionaries are enterprising. The high school MKs (missionary kids) going back to school after Christmas break were a priority use of MAF's limited fuel supply. So they sent in a small Cessna to pick the teens up. It was not scheduled to come from Sentani, so it didn't have our mail or supplies on board when it landed. Knowing that would be the case, someone arranged for a smallish Dani man (whose weight, added to the students' weight, would not exceed the plane's weight limit) to squeeze in with the kids and get out at the next stop. That station would get a plane from Sentani, and that flight would have our mail. Our Dani friend would get our mailbags, then hop on a plane to Bokondini in another area of the Dani tribe. From there he had only about a ten-hour walk over mountain trails back to Karubaga, carrying our precious mailbags. Dani people often walked distances like that over the mountain trails. It only took them one day, which was nothing to them, and this man was glad for the whole day's pay he would get.

Limited flights did not mean a lack of food. Flour, sugar, rice, and other things only available from the coast were routinely stock-piled for times when airplanes couldn't come in. We also had a good supply of vegetables we bought from the Danis—everything from their sweet potatoes, the anchor of their diet, plus other native vege-tables and Western veggies introduced by missionaries. Though the Danis ate some of those, their main motivation for planting them was to sell to us outsiders.

Sometimes Dani villagers also sold us parts of their indige-nous domesticated wild boar-like pigs. They also had chickens that missionaries had introduced earlier. These chickens ate whatever they could find as they roamed widely among gardens. They were strong; I never ate a tender one.

While I was at the Indonesian language school, I was in the cooking rotation. A wood stove and butchering chickens were part of my skills from childhood, so one Sunday I risked it—I cooked a local chicken. Rice mixed with sweet-sour sauce and extra pine-apple became stuffing. I took the chicken out of the oven to pour more sauce over it several times. The slow cooking and the added moisture made it edible—even good, though not what one would call tender. I was satisfied. And yes, just one chicken for the whole group. Meat was scarce, so it had to be served in petite portions. Everyone enjoyed our village chicken.

I had grown up with lots of meat. *Can I get used to so little?* I wondered. After several weeks, I did.

In one of my letters home, I wrote, "I've found cooking out here to be a ball. You must use your imagination and creative abili-ties. For instance, the other day I made us all sloppy joes. A simple enough matter at home, but not here. Right after breakfast, I had the Dani kitchen helpers cut up some tomatoes, onions, and green peppers that I boiled down for tomato sauce. I also had to have them bake the buns and grind up the meat!" (With a hand-cranked grinder, of course.)

How about unfamiliar food? Buah merah, for example.

Buah merah is the Indonesian name for red pandanus fruit, commonly called red fruit. About three feet long, it resembles a giant red ear of corn, filled with rows of seeds surrounded by a red oily substance. To prepare it, the tribal people steam it (usually in pits) to cook and loosen the capsules, scrape them off the core, then massage them in a carved wooden bowl to separate and remove the seeds from the pulp. The result looks like thick, oily tomato sauce.

Red fruit grows on both sides of Papua Island at only about 2,000 to 3,000 meters elevation. It is seasonal, rare, and has nutrition otherwise lacking in highlanders' diets. They crave it.

One day our kitchen workers cooked buah merah and were eating it in a small room off the kitchen. At first, I didn't know what was going on. I heard strange noises in there and saw this guy rush out with bright red stuff dripping from his hands. I peeked into the room, and there they were—squatted on the floor around a long shallow wooden bowl of the type they carve from the trunk of a tree. It was filled with vivid red sauce. They dipped into it with bits of banana leaves, then noisily sucked it off. That was the smacking noises I had heard.

"Buah merah" they explained.

"Oh, buah merah," I said, genuinely interested.

"Silakan makan" (Go ahead and eat).

That invitation didn't register quite as great an interest to me, but I thought it over for a second and decided to accept. I would never know what it tasted like until I tried it, and it would make something great to write home about.

Not having a piece of banana leaf, I just stuck in a finger up to the first knuckle and licked off as little as possible. I couldn't taste anything so licked off a bigger swipe. After the third try, I realized that the reason I couldn't find a flavor because it was—well—tasteless. The aftertaste is like unexciting, unseasoned tomato paste.

Ugh! I thought. *How can they love this?*

After a few years, I came to love it too. Maybe because my diet, which lacked fresh fruit and good oils, caused me, also, to crave them?

The relative isolation of Karubaga did not mean loneliness. With its six units of missionary staff (couples or singles) plus all the dozen students in the Indonesian language school, it was a supportive place. The quarter-mile walk to Sunday evening English language "church" service in a home was worth doing even in a pouring tropical rainstorm. Pounding rain on a tin roof could make it hard to hear, but even that was worth it. I found among my fellow missionaries a degree of dedication and tender-heartedness that I seldom saw in the US. Not that religious workers are, as some think, the highest group on the ladder of spirituality. But circumstances had deeply tested these missionaries' hearts for the Lord in unique ways. They had gone through years of tough experiences. Not that any of them were old. No missionary couples at Karubaga were empty nesters yet. But they had the wisdom and knowledge I needed. I learned all I could from them.

One learning opportunity occurred during a weekend I stayed with Jessie Williamson. She was a multi-certified nurse from Australia, and her house was next door to the two-bed hospital at Karubaga. That Saturday as I sat on her tiny porch cutting my hair—apparently riveting entertainment to on-looking Danis who seemed fascinated with unkinky hair—when I was suddenly upstaged. We all saw about a dozen men slowly wind their way down a path to Jessie's house supporting another man, especially his left arm. They stopped in front of the porch steps, and Jessie came out, talked with them in Dani for a second, and pointed to the hospital.

Turning to me, Jessie said, "He's broken his arm. Do you want to come to watch me set it?" I hesitated. *I'm only half-finished with my hair, but who is going to care, and when will I ever get another chance to see how to do this?*

When I stepped into the hospital, the poor guy was sitting on a stool in the entryway. One friend was at his left shoulder, pulling on his arm, and another was pulling his wrist the other direction. It looked like another two friends were there just for sympathy. They spoke to me in Dani. I didn't understand their words, but their gestures told me they wanted the door shut against the curious audience outside, so I obliged.

The patient just sat there while the two men pulled on his arm and blood dripped onto his leg. Jessie asked about the wound and was relieved that it was from a rock that had fallen on him, not from a protruding bone. Jessie had one of the man's friends hold his arm at the elbow so she could pull on his wrist to set the broken bone in his forearm.

After that, Jessie began a process so familiar to me from my childhood hospital days. She wrapped the arm in cotton, then soaked rolls of plaster bandage in water. As Jessie bent the man's arm at the elbow, he grunted and ground his teeth at the pain—an awful sound.

Jessie wound the plaster around the patient's arm, and plaster drips and dust began to coat the dark skin of his mostly naked body. "Your skin is turning white just like mine," Jessie said, but his face did not register humor. When Jessie finished with the plaster, she tied the man's arm up in a sling, gave his friends some instructions, handed him two aspirin (the only pain medicine given the whole time), and we left. Jessie wasn't cruel. Drugs were very scarce, and there was nothing else she could do.

That wasn't the only patient that day. A couple came with their two-week-old baby who had club feet, a common condition there. An Australian friend of Jessie's had sent her some braces to correct the problem, so she had what she needed to straighten the baby's feet.

Another time, a pregnant woman came with the baby turned the wrong way inside her. Jessie laid the woman down right there on the grass of the yard and with her hands turned the baby around. Jessie often did things like that. Things only a doctor would do in normal circumstances, but there was no doctor at Karubaga yet, and she had to help as she could.

"Do what you can do"—a lesson learned.

Chapter 27

WHICH TRIBE?

Before I went from Sentani to Karubaga, the RBMU Field Executive Committee asked me to take advantage of the knowledge of missionaries passing through. The committee didn't know which ministry needed my skills most and neither did I. Teaching? Translating? Children's work? Writing? I needed to find out everything I could about the needs in the various tribal areas.

There are over 270 languages on the Indonesian half of the island. RBMU (now World Team), worked in several tribal areas. In those places, very few, if any, of the people knew even a limited amount of the national language, Indonesian. One had to communicate in the local language. Wherever I served, I would need to know that tribe's language. Some of their vernacular inventories of words were distantly related to another tribal language, but most were not. Each people group also had cultural distinctions. Only a few groups had the advantage of literacy classes so they could read and write their own words and had started a Bible translation. Even now as I write this, fewer than a handful of all those languages have a complete Bible translation. The question for me was where I should work and doing what.

Much of the information I needed came from the Dani evangelists working in both mountain and coastal areas. For example, some people in Sela Valley, east of Korupun, had asked for Bible teachers, but other Sela people threatened to kill any evangelists. That was a genuine threat, but six Dani men—five evangelists and one medic—decided they would go. These men were going into a potentially dangerous area, leaving wives and children behind until they could build homes, but they were willing to do it for the Lord. The plan was to fly to Wamena and trek from there to Sela, which would take seven to ten days. Jacques Teeuwen, a missionary in the eastern highland mountains, asked them if they would rather wait for a plane connection closer to Sela. They said, "No. These people are dying without Jesus. We are not doing this for ourselves. We are doing it for God. We will go now. We will walk."

As it turned out, there was a medical emergency in the eastern highlands which required an airplane, so four of them could fly from Wamena and be dropped off at Korupun, which was the nearest airstrip to Sela, which had no airstrip. From Korupun it was only a ten-hour walk to Sela. It seemed to me that a ten-hour walk instead of a several-day walk was the Lord's special reward for their willingness of heart.

The other two men needed to walk the entire way from Karubaga because the plane could not take more than four. Who would walk and who would fly was a voluntary choice. They knew the walk would be two or more weeks. The way was steep and slippery and through areas that spoke languages strange to them. Still, they wanted to go, and two of the men volunteered to walk.

Where would I end up? Could I handle primitive living and isolation if I go to a rugged and remote spot?

One day Dave Martin, the RBMU field director, came to Karubaga to give us some orientation about the work the mission was doing in Irian Jaya. The field conference was only a month away. During our conference, all but newly arrived members would discuss and decide our allocations to specific places and work roles. Dave spread out a map to show us RBMU's locations on both north and south coasts in the lowlands on either side of the mountain range that stretched from east to west across the island, and the work in those mountains.

As I heard about the work of the Dani evangelists and Western missionaries, Korupun stood out the most. I told only the Lord.

I confessed, "Lord, I think I know what I want, but please use my field leaders to reveal the right place for me."

The night of Dave's visit to Karubaga, he carefully asked me where I thought I might like to work. Neither one of us wanted to prejudice the other with our ideas, but after dancing around a bit in our conversation, we discovered that we both thought Korupun might be the place I would fit best.

During those months of language study at Karubaga, I had been drawn to information about the Korupun Valley and beyond, where the Kimyal tribe lived. This tribe covers a 200 square mile area of small valleys in the eastern highlands. The area is divided approximately in half by a high ridge of mountains that runs north and south, creating two valley systems. One stretches from Korupun to the southern lowlands and the other ranges from Sela south to the lowlands. The people of the Korupun Valley were the culture-shapers of the western half of the tribe. East, on the other side of the ridge, the Sela Valley was the dominant force of that half of the tribe. Between Korupun and Sela is one of the highest mountains in Papua.

Within the Korupun half of the Kimyal tribe, there had recently been a small breakthrough of interest in God but also strong opposition to any talk about Jesus. More Bible teaching was a crucial need, and that required proper language analysis and Scripture translation. That would be my contribution—building on the work already done.

Ten years before I arrived in Irian Jaya, Phil Masters, the Prairie Bible Institute alum who had been killed in Papua during my senior year at PBI, and Bruno deLeeuw, missionary to the Yali tribe east of the Kimyal people, were the first-ever white people to make contact with any of the Kimyal tribe.

I learned that in 1963, Phil and Bruno walked for days east from Ninia (Yali territory), hoping to find this tribe Yalis spoke of. They did find the Korupun Valley and its people. Those Kimyals seemed to accept the men, so Phil and Bruno chose an airstrip site in the Korupun Valley, bought that land, and began to build an airstrip.

For that work, airplanes dropped wheelbarrow parts to assemble and shovels. The project took months.

Finally, the airstrip was finished and approved by MAF. Phyliss and the children joined Phil at Korupun in 1964. With the airstrip work behind him, Phil put more time into learning the Kimyal language. He did initial grammar analysis, developed a trial writing system, and even wrote some early draft Bible portion translations. He also began preaching in various villages on Sundays. Response to Phil's teaching was sluggish.

In September 1968, Phil and his friend Stan Dale, a colleague of Bruno's at Ninia, went on a trek into a Yali area where there was no Bible teacher. By that time, Phil had written down some of what he knew about the Kimyal language, but much of his knowledge was only in his mind. When the two of them were killed on the journey, that knowledge was lost to other missionaries when Phil died.

After her husband's death, Phyllis went back to Karubaga, where she and Phil had worked before. To fill the void of a missionary at Korupun, in 1969, Paul and Kathryn Kline agreed to leave their work at Karubaga and go to Korupun, the only place in Kimyal territory with an airstrip, until someone linguistically trained could go long-term to translate the Bible into Kimyal. Stan Dale's wife decided it was best to leave Ninia and move back to Australia with her children.

In 1974, during the time I was in language school at Karubaga, there was no missionary at Korupun. The Klines were in the US on leave, and Bruce McLeay, a New Zealander, was assigned to Korupun, but he was home to get married. Bruce planned to be the church planter and developer of Kimyal church leaders, but he was not a linguist.

As Dave and I talked, we both felt I was a good fit for those linguistic jobs, but it would be official only if everyone agreed to it during our field conference in a month.

In the meantime, I was still at Karubaga and still in the Indonesian language school.

Chapter 28

A DELAY IN PLANS

Fresh mountain air poured in through the open window, the door, and the cracks in the walls of my cabin in Karubaga. The breeze carried scents of tall grass, trees, gardens, and today, smoke. Several columns of smoke rose from funeral pyres on mountainsides—the Dani way of handling the bodies of their dead. Influenza had hit them, and it spread rapidly.

It's no wonder they are vulnerable targets of flu. How is it that the children can ignore the flies that buzz around and land on the thick yellow goo always plastered between nose and mouth? And their chronic coughs—adults seem to be healthier, but their lives are short. Few reach age fifty, and now flu is killing many of those and the babies. How in the world can we instruct these people about germs they can't see and hygiene practices that seem to dishonor the customs of their ancestors? At least they have accepted the making of small hut-style toilets instead of just jumping into high grass to relieve themselves.

The missionaries soon ran out of penicillin and sulfa, the only drugs available then for flu, and resorted to giving only aspirins. As more people died, more wailing and more smoke rose throughout the valley. Fifty-four Danis died in Karubaga that year, and Karubaga wasn't the worst-hit area.

I got the flu too. It had been years since I went to bed due to sickness. Gloria, one of the single gals who worked at Karubaga, invited me to her house to recover. She warned me, "Out here you have to make sure you are completely well before working again, or you'll relapse."

I thought, *Nah, I can push through.*

Nope. I tried that and ended up sick all over again.

Gloria told me, "When I first came here, I got the flu every month. You'll have to build your resistance to these pesky foreign germs, as I did."

While I was sick and recuperating at Gloria's, I had a visit from Bruno and Marlys deLeeuw. They worked at Ninia with the Yali people, the tribe west of the Kimyals and north of a recently contacted lowland tribe called the Somohai. Besides telling me about that tribe, Bruno also told me what he had recently seen of the Kimyals.

"In March, John Wilson and I trekked from Ninia through the Seng and Solo Valleys of the Yali tribe and then to Korupun, the same route Phil and I took in 1963 for the first contact with the Kimyal tribe, and the route, in reverse, that Stan and Phil took in 1968 when they were killed. John and I had a good trek. As we entered Korupun, the gateway to the Kimyal area, we saw a lot of interest in the gospel. They are ready for a linguist and Bible translator, and there is a great need for one."

I felt a tug on my heart. Later I confided to Gloria, "I think God arranged this chance for the deLeeuws to visit me. If I had been in my cabin and in classes, I would not have had that conversation. I feel even more strongly that maybe working with the Kimyal people at Korupun is God's place for me. Our field conference is just a couple weeks away—we'll see."

Language school used the conference buildings, so we all took time off to get everything ready for the coming group. I moved to a conference complex cabin I shared with Gail. Gloria's extra space was already reserved, and my former cabin was needed for a married couple.

Finally, the day came when conference flights started coming in—up to five planes a day, including Commander loads, much more than the small Cessnas could carry. At that time, most of MAF's planes were Cessna 185s outfitted with a cargo pod under the cabin section. If passengers were small and had little baggage, the 185s could carry six. MAF also had a few Cessna 206s, which could hold seven passengers and had a more powerful engine to maneuver around mountains. The biggest and strongest was the Commander. It held about the same number of passengers as the smaller Cessnas but could take a lot more cargo. All were single-engine airplanes, our sole source of transportation besides walking, and we knew each one and their pilots well.

The conference started with a welcome and introduction meeting. Not all members had met the newcomers yet. After those introductions, interviews with the executive committee and physical check-ups occupied the first day or two.

During my interview with the executive committee (ExCom), I tried to control my nerves, but I did fidget a bit, and my heart pounded.

"Do you have a preference for your assignment?" they asked.

"I feel most drawn to the need at Korupun and beyond, among the Kimyals. But I will agree with whatever you and the field in general decide."

Their focused expressions told me that they were interested and accepting, but they were noncommittal. The final decision was up to a vote of field members.

The ExCom interview over, Dr. Liz Cousens did my physical exam. She almost forgot the basics in her fascination with my muscle compensation and how my existing muscles had taken over for lost ones.

"May I satisfy my curiosity with some muscle tests?" she asked. Then, when she got back to the usual questions, she couldn't remember what she'd done already. "Have I checked your ears?"

That took my mind off the pending vote and helped me relax.

Four days later, the field vote came. "Congratulations. Your place is Korupun. The only question is when you can go."

I needed a house of my own long-term, and while I got set up there, either the Klines or the McLeays or both also had to be on site. ExCom would not allow a single woman to start her work in a tribe on her own. Neither couple would be at Korupun midyear to build a house for me or for me to stay with during the build. The Indonesian language school wouldn't finish until July. How all this would work out wasn't clear.

Not all was business though. Saturday night we had an honest-to-goodness candlelight Thanksgiving banquet. Yes, Thanksgiving in April. Why not? We only got together once a year, and dress-up occasions were almost nonexistent otherwise. We had duck, chicken, cranberry sauce, and cranberry jelly (from cans), buns, giblet gravy, mashed potatoes, candied sweet potatoes, and other vegetables. Dessert was a choice of cherry, mincemeat, or pumpkin pie. The men all wore suits, and the ladies wore long dresses. We had taped background music and a nice horn-of-plenty display. What a morale booster for missionaries living in isolated, lonely spots across the island.

Another boost of morale was the ladies' prayer-and-share time. As I listened to the stories of joy, disappointment, struggle, failure, and victory and how God helped them in it all, I thought, *I wish people at home could see that missionary wives and singles are ordinary women.*

Missionary women have the same basic temptations, weaknesses, strengths, and emotions as all women. All that plus the added dimension of having to face those things alone with the Lord, sometimes even if they have a husband. They can't get on the phone or hop in the car to talk things over with a trusted friend. But at the conference, I heard a real note of joy, victory, and acceptance among the gals. They seemed very happy with their situation and their service.

A few days later: "Elinor, we have a suggestion for you." It was a member of the language committee. "When you finish this Indonesian language course, would you be willing to teach the next one? At least the first three months of it? There will be four or five new couples by then and some others who haven't had a chance yet to take a course in Indonesian. It will run mid-September to mid-December. ExCom okayed the idea."

I thought, *Yikes! I've done well in Indonesian, but not exceptionally well!* I knew, though, that there seemed to be no one else available to do it. The teacher of our group had come from her normal missionary work to teach us. I also knew that since the other Korupun personnel wouldn't be back when I finished this course, I couldn't go to Korupun right away anyway. I would have time to visit other places to get a view of our broader work. That would help me to see the work at Korupun in the context of the whole field.

But the language school job would mean not just teaching but also assigning housing, ordering food, hiring kitchen help, overseeing them, and more. I was new to all this and not an organizer. I wasn't sure I could do it.

I pondered the request for a few days and answered, "Yes, I will do the first three months. After that, the Klines will be back, and I can move to Korupun. But I wish you could find someone else to coordinate it and let me just teach."

Friday night of the conference was Fun Night when whoever wanted to make a fool of themselves in front of everyone else was free to do so. One of the men, Dr. Liz's husband, Graham Cousens, asked me to help him in a skit.

Jurgen Otterbach, a German butcher by former trade, was patiently waiting for Annegret, his fiancé, to get legal permission to come to Irian Jaya. Jurgen was six four and weighed 250–280 pounds. Graham asked me, all of four seven, to be Jurgen. Graham asked the slightly rotund missionary Gaylord to be Annegret. Graham would be the preacher at their wedding. So Graham stole Jurgen's jacket, hat, shoes, and knife belt and dressed me up. Gaylord wore a sheet for a dress, a mosquito-net veil, and a wig. Jurgen was easy to imitate; he had very distinctive mannerisms and accent. And Graham, as the preacher, did a perfect imitation of Mr. Oliver, our British conference speaker at our evening services.

Chapter 29

TROUBLING NEWS

Once again Karubaga Valley filled with the noise and hustle-bustle of airplanes coming and going as the conference closed, and everyone returned to their work. I settled back into Indonesian language learning, planning for teaching the next new class and my eventual move to Korupun.

Then, over the two-way radio, we heard, "There has been trouble at Nipsan. The Indonesian evangelist who usually checks in by radio four days a week while the Dutch Reformed missionary is on leave missed the check-in. MAF flew over Nipsan to survey things. No plane can land. Boulders and tree trunks litter the airstrip, and there is a trench dug across it. Warriors with bows and arrows sit on the approach end, ready to shoot at any plane that comes close. They made threatening gestures when the plane came in low. Hundreds of warriors are milling around. The missionary's house is burned. Destruction is everywhere; there is no evidence of where the fourteen national evangelists might be."

All of this especially interested me. Nipsan was a related language to Kimyal, less than forty miles of challenging trail away from Korupun but on the north slope of the Papua's east-to-west mountain range. Those factors meant there was no threat to Korupun, but it was a sobering reality of the state of resistance to the gospel's entering these tribal areas.

The first Indonesian military party sent in to investigate disappeared. Two weeks later, one of the national evangelists arrived at a safe area and told what happened in the attack:

"When the warriors started to attack, the radio man told the other evangelists to run. He would try to radio for help and try to talk the attackers out of their murderous plans, but they wouldn't listen to him. They tore the roof and one wall off the radio building to get at the man."

Later all that was found of him and one other evangelist were their heads. None of the others were found, except one wounded woman who escaped.

What are the implications of this to the work at Korupun? I asked myself. *Seasoned missionaries say it won't encourage a similar revolt at Korupun. But the recent spiritual breakthrough there is shaky. News of the Nipsan affair could slow down that progress. I hear that chief Wamai at Korupun, who for so long has held his people back from turning to the Lord, has done a symbolic fetish burning, destroying those ties to the spirit ancestors. But it is doubtful that he is truly following the Lord yet. What happened at Nipsan could push him and the other wavering people away from God. Or will it have the opposite effect?*

I didn't have long to ponder those things before I had to decide whether to accept two invitations for the two-week break that would come between the course I was taking and the one I would be leading. I needed the vacation I was due. One offer was to visit the Cousens family at Soba in the eastern highlands, just fifteen minutes west of Korupun by plane. *It's a different valley and language from Korupun, but some things would be similar—a good introduction,* I thought. The other request was from Don and Carol Richardson at Kamur in the hot, steamy south coast jungle.

I accepted both invitations. I felt that splitting my time and seeing the settings and cultures of different tribes could help my understanding of the province.

Chapter 30

A TRIP TO SOBA

I was the only passenger as the plane took off from Karubaga to fly east to Soba. I saw the details of villages I couldn't see from the ground. The neatly laid out Dani villages were made from about six huts clustered together, not necessarily in rows but not haphazardly either. They were always free of debris. Often, not a village but just two huts perched on a mountainside, and sometimes, only one. Past the Swart Valley, the sun shone in full force and seemed to highlight the colors of the scene. The lush green mountains were dotted with the clean straw color of the huts and the reddish overturned soil, all against the background of a vast, deep blue sky with fleecy white clouds. Though we were out of Swart Valley, we weren't above the mountains yet.

We turned east and followed a mountain pass to Bokondini and then flew south and east, heading for the Grand Baliem Valley. Soba, Ninia, and Korupun all lie east of the Baliem, on the south slope of the mountain range that cuts east–west across the island.

As we neared the Baliem Valley, the mountains became sharper. There was less vegetation, the population appeared to thin out, and the mountain pass narrowed. We came into the valley with a change of scenery so sudden it was like a different slide projected on the screen of the earth. No longer were we in a narrow valley with a rugged, uneven floor. Now we were over a broad valley with mountains in the distance on either side and a valley floor almost perfectly flat. The mood of the river changed too. No longer was it tumbling through narrow valleys. It was a muddy, sluggish, winding river, almost curling back on itself in places.

To my inexperienced eyes, the broad valley floor looked less populated than the Swart Valley, but it may have seemed that way because it was garden after garden after garden. Instead of pig fences, now the only lines were the outlines and paths of the gardens. These were laid out geometrically but not necessarily in straight rows. Sometimes they would bend in on each other in shapes that made the gardens look for all the world like giant slabs of ancient Coptic writing.

How can a small population consume all the produce from this huge valley? I wondered. Later I learned that four stages of gardens grow at the same time. The first stage is the old, spent gardens which are not yet worked up for planting a new crop. Next come gardens that are worked and showing just-planted sweet potato vines. Next to them are gardens that are well on their way but not yet ready for harvest. The final step is harvesting the mature gardens. In this way, there is year-round harvest, planting, and cultivating.

The city of Wamena seemed out of place in the broad primitive valley. Established in the early days of the Dutch government on this side of New Guinea, blocks of houses were in perfect squares. The city was not all that large but seemed so in the middle of an otherwise "empty" valley. MAF had a base there that served the missionaries of the eastern highlands and south coast.

East past the Baliem Valley we again flew over mountains. They were steeper than any I had seen. Ridges were sharper than those in the Swart Valley, and the western slopes were almost bald. I imagined that if any trees tried to grow there, their branches wouldn't clear the mountainside. In many places, bare rock showed through or landslides had wiped clean great slabs of a mountain. Then I saw garden plots on seemingly vertical mountain faces. *How do they do that? It looks impossible!*

The pass leading to Soba was very narrow, judging by the distance between the wing on my side of the plane and the mountains. We descended to the correct altitude before we could see the airstrip. Below us was a big dip in the ground, then a rise. This creates an illusion—you think you are above the end of the airstrip (which drops off into a gorge) when you are below it. Pilots had to approach and land using instrument readings. I didn't know those things—I just noticed that we turned a sharp left then touched down. Later Graham Cousens told me, "Often the pilots have to gun the engine at the last minute to hop up onto the strip."

Soba sits about 1,000 to 1,500 feet above the river, with mountains close around and no level ground anywhere. The Cousens family were the only missionaries there, and their house was past the upper end of the airstrip, further up through a few trees and a yard. Behind their home, the mountains steeply rose again. If it were not for the fact that you could see a little way down the valley from the top end of the strip, you could feel closed in.

"Korupun is even more closed in," Liz said.

Well, I thought, *if it is this beautiful, I won't mind.*

As soon as I stepped through the door of the Cousens' house, the children (four-year-old Deborah and two-year-old Steven) wanted me to read to them and draw pictures. I had brought a guitar that came in one of my shipped barrels, but I had not had time to play at Karubaga. When they saw the guitar, the Cousens children also wanted me to play it and sing with them and otherwise entertain. It was entertainment for me too.

On Saturday we went on a picnic up over the mountain behind the house and down the other side to the river of the next valley. I wanted to walk the trail myself. By then I was strong enough to climb even that steep mountain if I had a helper on each side to hang onto, but it had rained so hard the night before that the trail was thick goo. Slippery, sticky stuff. So again I got a ride on shoulders, this time Hupla (the tribe at Soba) as well as Dani shoulders. Because I wasn't walking, I didn't need to watch the trail. I could look up at the crisp green mountains or blue sky, or down in the valley, or at the little village across the ridge from us.

When my carriers and I got to the bottom of the steep, twisted path, we sat down to wait for the others. We were in front of the only hut in that small valley. One little pig was tied outside it, and there were some children there. Did they live there, or were they just pig-tenders? Either way, we provided them with the day's enter-tainment as the picnic spot was only forty feet away.

We sat to eat on an almost flat grassy area beside the river where the sharply descending water roared over boulders and splashed plants growing along its shores. All those giant rocks had a coat of tan lime. At one spot they made a sort of natural pool where Deborah and Steven splashed and laughed.

After we finished our sandwiches, Graham wanted me to see the small waterfall in the river higher up. Once again I rode on shoulders and off we went, sometimes wading through icy cold water, sometimes stepping from boulder to boulder to cross the river, then up a steep bank and across again in another place. Finally, we got to the waterfall. It was just fifteen feet high and very narrow. The thick jungle hanging over it made it look like one of those paintings that someone made up. It was that beautiful.

On the way home, we stopped at the crest of the mountain before descending the other side. We could see another waterfall from there, and tall tropical highland trees on the other side of the valley—again a painting no one would believe.

During the next week, Graham flew to another station. One day while he was gone, a call came on the radio for Dr. Liz to go to yet another station to tend several wounded men. Some men who were not followers of Jesus had surprise-attacked a group of Christians. The chief, a Christian, was dead from his wounds. The station, Pasima, where Dutch missionaries Peter and Nel Akse lived, was a short five-minute flight from Soba.

While Liz packed the medical gear she would need, I waited by the radio to answer any calls. I had heard transmissions via those radios but had never talked on one so I was nervous as I listened for a summons for Soba. I knew that anyone anywhere on the island might be eavesdropping, and I didn't know all the unique radio vocabulary. I did know, though, the call signs of most of the airplanes, and we all sprang into overdrive when I confirmed that I heard, "Soba, Mike Charlie Alpha. ETA ten minutes."

Before long we were at Pasima. Before we got out of the plane, we heard wailing. The enemy had put the body of the chief where his friends could retrieve it and carry it the two hours home to Pasima. The dead man was lying in the Akse's front yard, where hundreds of people gathered to mourn. The government had sent police there too. Their khaki and green uniforms and their guns added an ominous air to the scene.

Nel Akse's face showed relief as we climbed out of the plane. The chief had been a personal friend, and there was no other missionary woman there with whom to share her grief.

We learned what had started the fighting. The men of this and other tribes had specially long hair and were proud of it. The government said they must all cut their hair. The reason wasn't clear, but the men from the nearest village, one that was open to the gospel, wanted to cooperate, so they cut their hair and went to the other settlement to cut hair there too. Those men didn't want their hair cut, so they hid in the bushes, let the Pasima men enter their village, then surrounded and attacked them. The hair issue was an excuse. For a long time, they had wanted to kill that chief. Several men jumped on him and hit him while the rest of his party ran.

When we got to Pasima, some of the women showed Liz and me the chief's wounds. He had taken an ax or two in the head, an arrow in the throat, and had other injuries in his back, chest, and stomach.

The other wounded men would not arrive until the next morning after the police secured the trail going back.

This attack happened not long after the Nipsan incident on the north slope of the mountains where locals killed Indonesian evangelists and destroyed the airstrip. I asked one of the policemen if police were still at Nipsan. "No, they were chased out," he said.

All this killing . . . Might I face a day when I see the body of a friend killed by enemies of the gospel?

Chapter 31

KAMUR: I VISIT THE LOWLANDS

I returned from Soba to Karubaga with a lot to think about as I prepared for the next six weeks or so. I had two weeks before I left for my visit to the Richardsons at Kamur on the south coast and then briefly visit Korupun. I had not expected to start Indonesian classes right after that, but the field language committee told me that the McLeays, who would one day join me at Korupun, and another couple would soon arrive in Irian Jaya. "Would you start them with Indonesian lessons after your Korupun visit? There may be a couple with MAF too," the field language committee requested.

I agreed to do that. I was not going to have as much organizing time as I originally thought, so I wanted to get as much done as I could before I left for Kamur and Korupun.

I gave MAF my flight requests for going to Kamur, Korupun, and back to Karubaga. A flight scheduler would coordinate all people and cargo flight requests to make the flights as efficient and cost-effective as possible. Sometimes they couldn't fit a requested flight in, and you had to try again the next week.

I hoped my requests would work, then at once started lining up all the Dani workers we would need for the Indonesian language course. I couldn't speak Dani, and they could speak little Indonesian, so I needed the help of someone who knew at least a little of both languages.

Gail had taken the same Indonesian course I had and was now studying Dani. Helping me would help her. She was always up for anything. We were both relative newcomers, learning as we went along. Gail knew how to relieve stress for me.

A fun interlude was when I got to explore the Karubaga Valley trails on the back of Gail's motorbike. A plane had brought the bike in two weeks earlier, but Gail had no idea how to drive one. The closest she had come to driving one was when she sat on this one in the showroom in Australia where she bought it. We had a wobbly good time as Gail practiced and good laughs at our close calls. Our goal was to go to the top of the mountain after practicing with short trips. I know what you're thinking: "Were you nuts?" We eventually made it.

Soon it was time for my visit to the Richardsons at Kamur, a much-needed use of my allotted vacation time. This week would serve both as a break and aid my comprehension of the broad scope of the island's geography which shaped the tribal cultures along with our strategies for working among these diverse tribes. This gut-level "boots-on-the-ground" understanding of each other's working situation was a big part of what bound us together, and feeling that bond was part of what gave steady strength in the tough times.

I would pay the fare for my vacation trip to Kamur. Going to Korupun was part of my orientation to my future work there, so other funds paid for that.

As on my earlier flight to the eastern highlands to visit Soba, from Karubaga we flew through the Bokondini pass to get to the South Gap. That's where we hit trouble. A big cloud blocked the pass, so we made a sharp turn back. I felt like I was sitting parallel to the horizon. So did my stomach. We circled higher and higher to get over the clouds, and when it seemed we had, we caught a down draft. "An elevator," Ken, the pilot, said as he handed me a sick sack. I didn't need it, though we circled three more times before we finally got above the cloud. That thirty-five minutes got us ten minutes from Karubaga.

Our first destination on the south coast was a village called Yawsakor, which sits beside a wide river. We landed on a ground

KAMUR: I VISIT THE LOWLANDS

airstrip there. As the pilot and missionaries unloaded that plane with the supplies it had brought to Yawsakor, I transferred to a floatplane for my flight to Kamur which had no landing strip other than the river.

The takeoff was the smoothest I had yet experienced. The river was calm as we gained speed to lift off. The splash of water off the floats and the growing rooster-tail before takeoff reminded me of a speedboat.

On our way to Kamur, we needed to land at a small riverside village and check on a Dani evangelist's wife. Don Richardson had heard from others that she was quite sick. News of such things could travel up and down the rivers by boat or even on foot through the jungle.

This, my first water landing, was as smooth as the takeoff. As we coasted toward shore, people ran to us from the eight huts. Each one was rectangular, not round as in the mountains. They were on stilts off the ground and did not look very sturdy.

The villagers here appeared distinctly different from the mountain dwellers. The women's reed skirts had more style than mountain skirts; they had a kind of bustle in the back. The men traditionally wore nothing. A few of the older ones still chose that. The others wore shreds of shorts that weren't much better than the traditional look.

As we drifted toward shore, a teenage boy came out of the village and onto an eight-inch diameter log that jutted over the river. He grabbed a wing of the plane so we wouldn't drift back out again. Bob, the pilot, got out and stood on a float to talk to the Dani evangelist about his wife. How sick was she? Would she come with us to get help? Yes, she was quite ill, but no, she wouldn't agree to go. So Bob got back in his seat, the boy gave us a shove, and we drifted back to the middle of the river and took off again.

I gained a new respect for the Dani evangelists in areas like that. We Western missionaries at least had communication radios;

they didn't. And they lived right in the middle of village life in a way we couldn't.

A short flight took us to Kamur. The Richardson's house was near four relatively large villages.

Crowds of Sawis joined the Richardsons at their dock to meet us. I noticed that Sawi features were more slight than those of the highland people. The Sawis' bodies are long and slim, whereas highlanders are more round and squat. Also, the Sawis didn't have the potbellies that mountain tribes carried. Sawi people also had skin diseases not seen in the mountains. These diseases made the skin look flaky and scaly.

Culturally, the Sawi people seemed to feel duty-bound to greet visitors with at least a handshake and a "Konahare," their greeting word. To avoid getting their skin diseases, I had to wash my hands after each greeting session. My hands became well-scrubbed during my time there.

Whereas Danis carried their babies on their shoulders, Sawis carried babies on their backs, piggy-back style. For babies too young to hang on, mothers made small woven seats that held them on. Amazingly early they could hang on by themselves.

I wondered, *How can a tiny baby do that?*

One baby had his arms around his mother's neck and his feet around the mother's stomach while she stood and paddled down the river. A woman's food-gathering canoe was too narrow to sit in, even had she wanted to. I watched another mother paddle her little dugout craft to the middle of the river, stop, and standing with baby clinging to her back, lean over the side and fill a bamboo section with water—all without causing the boat to tip.

Do the Dani evangelists' wives learn to do that? I couldn't.

On Saturday, Don took Carol and me in their canoe—large enough to sit in—down the river to the site where some men were making one of three huge ironwood dugout canoes Don had hired them to make.

As we went along, the only reminder of civilization was the sound of the outboard motor, but it couldn't drown out the loud calls of the birds in the jungle.

Finally, our guide pointed and said, "There. There is where it is—the boat they are making."

Really? I thought. *I don't see a path. Except for the ends of a couple of boats, it looks like the rest of the river.*

Don turned our boat toward the spot, and as soon as we got under the brush, we saw a niche where Don could park our canoe. He said, "This fellow says the canoe tree is close, but that could mean just a little way or a long way. It doesn't look like a good path." Protruding tree roots and vines at the right height to trip a person crossed the muddy track. "If you want to go in a bit, you are welcome. Keep checking for leeches around your ankles."

Carol's under-her-breath comment, "Oh dear, I forgot a razor for snake bites," deflated my pioneer spirit. We told Don, "Go ahead. We'll try to see if we can make it."

The trail was impossible; we soon turned back. Mosquitoes followed us back out of the jungle and into our canoe. We sat in the dugout and waved whatever we could find at the mosquitoes, hoping that would keep some from landing on us.

I was relieved to finally see Don come back. He got in the canoe and took us up the river to the site of the second future houseboat canoe. Don planned to use the houseboat to reach and stay a day or two at villages up and down the river.

My ears tuned in to the creature noises from unseen animals and insects all around us. It was like a Tarzan soundtrack. On the river ride home, we passed a great white egret sitting in a tree, undisturbed by the noise of our boat.

What beauty. But as much as I love all this, I think I see why God pointed me to work in the highlands. It won't be easy, but living on one of these rivers this way would require even more from my body.

Chapter 32

FIRST VISIT TO KORUPUN

I left Kamur knowing that two more river landings lay between it and the mountains that held Korupun.

Between Kamur and the first landing, Kawem, the tall broccoli-like trees gave way to giant ferns which gave way to tall waving swamp grass along a narrow, dirty river. At Kawem I got out of the plane and looked around. The Kayagar people there are a different language group from the Sawis, but their appearance was so similar I couldn't tell any difference. They were also just as friendly. So many people tried to help me get between the plane and the dock that I thought I might land in the water.

Safely on land, I saw that the crowd was curious about me. Some smiled, some stared, and some showed almost shocked astonishment.

Someone explained, "It is good for these people to see a person like you. It shows that not all white people are a tower of strength and health. They think only their people have afflictions. It's good for them to see that is not true."

From Kawem we landed on choppy water at Yawsakor where we switched to a wheel plane and were on our way to Wamena. The next day would be my long-anticipated first landing at Korupun and my first glimpse of the Kimyal people.

Kathryn Kline was also waiting at Wamena for the next morning's flight to Korupun, where she and Paul still lived. Bad weather delayed our takeoff, something I came to almost expect of flights to and from Korupun. My seat was the little one in the plane's tail, with cargo piled all around me so that I barely had enough room. That was just the first of many rides in the tail.

We were soon in a section of mountains east beyond Soba—mountains I'd never seen before. As we got deeper into the highlands, more clouds appeared. Then I saw something else new to me. We were above thin clouds, and the sun projected our shadow onto them. Encircling that shadow was a circular rainbow, sometimes two. Beautiful!

The symbol of God's care and protection around us.

Peace settled into my heart.

Thirty minutes from Wamena we approached the Korupun Valley. Many eastern highlands airstrips end at a sheer drop-off. Korupun did, too, but the approach to Korupun is unique. First, we circled high above to check that the airstrip was OK—a tight circle because it's a narrow valley. When we made our approach at near landing altitude, it looked like the right wing would scrape the trees on the side of the sheer mountain beside us. We couldn't see the airstrip until the pilot made a sudden left turn, and there it was, right in front of us. Land or crash. The stall warning squawked as the flaps slowed us just before the wheels hit their target.

It seemed streams of people on the paths along the sides of the airstrip tried to outrun us to the top end. Hoots, whistles, and strange-to-me language sounds greeted us as we got out of the plane. At last, I was at Korupun, if even for just a visit.

Experienced Kimyals unloaded the plane quickly so John, the pilot, could take off before the weather closed us down again. What looked like the noisy chaos of a hundred very verbal bosses and no peons got the job done quickly and well. Though I knew neither language, I could hear that Kimyal had a distinctly different sound from Dani.

OK—my linguistic classes taught me that I will learn to distinguish words. I sure hope so. This sounds like run-on nonsense!

At the top of the airstrip, I met Bruce and Judy McLeay for the first time. They would go to Karubaga for the Indonesian language school that I would teach, but after that, it would be them and me at Korupun without the Klines.

During the two weeks of my visit, I worked on house plans, wrote letters to family and friends (a never-ending task), and Judy and I took walks all over that valley, so tightly wrapped by high mountains. Each time, as soon as we left the house, Kimyal children rushed to join us. "Ane na girig," one would say, and pick up a rock. Another would point to a flower and say, "eisa'." Or one would point to one of the many waterfalls and say, "Mag musu." They laughed at our attempts to repeat what they said. I laughed too. I quickly learned the word "mag," water. The encircling mountain cliffs were so close and steep that the sounds of the waterfalls and the big river were constant background music.

Many days the weather was rainy and cold or foggy and cold, making the wet clay soil slippery mush. On rainy days I stayed inside, wrapped myself in a blanket near the fire, and wrote letters, read, or drew house plans.

We Westerners are not able to survive in the smoky, dirty, no-room-to-stand-up eight-foot diameter, drafty, round huts that the mountain tribes live in. Diseases would soon kill us as they did many of the villagers. Infant mortality was high and life expectancy was less than age fifty.

As I sketched plans for my small house, I included a wood-burning space heater in my tiny sitting area as well as a wood-burning cookstove in the kitchen. I would need both.

Life at Korupun would not be like life at Karubaga. This valley was higher, colder, foggier, rainier, and more tightly enclosed than Karubaga. Also, even from my short time with them, I sensed that Kimyals were more openly expressive than Danis. Though Karubaga was the more familiar place for me then, Korupun would become home.

After my visit, I left with many questions.

Privately I wondered, *How will it be to live here? How will I learn the language, come to know individuals, their tribal ways, live with the cold, damp, and dimness, and how to get from village to village on these mountain paths?*

Chapter 33

I BEGIN LIFE AT KORUPUN

As I returned to Karubaga and began teaching Indonesian to new missionaries, Paul Kline worked on building my house at Korupun.

Paul arranged for a portable sawmill to be flown to Korupun, fixed the motor, hired Kimyal men to carry the sawmill pieces to the mill site an hour up a mountain, and then he assembled it. There in the forest, the Kimyals had felled trees weeks earlier, so sawing began as soon as the sawmill arrived. Men carried the sawn and planed boards down the mountain to the house site Paul had bought and prepared. Just those things took months.

This milled timber was for framing, rafters, floors, and a few interior walls. Everything else in the house was poles or palm bark. My house was twenty-by-thirty feet and one-and-a-half stories high. The kitchen, dining area, sitting area, bathroom, bedroom, and office were on the main floor; upstairs held a clothes-drying area and two small guest rooms. When planes flying overhead got closed in by weather, the pilot and any passengers needed a place to sleep for the night.

While Paul worked on my house, I was back at Karubaga. Besides the job of coordinating and teaching the language courses, also weighing on me was a problem I had not expected. The problem centered around certain other missionaries' perception of me as a dependent disabled person. Just a couple of them, but I felt it. I saw resentment in their attitudes, and it rattled me.

I had worked hard through childhood and adolescence to show that I could be an independent and productive adult. I hadn't expected this. These individuals feared that my physical limitations would cause them or their husbands to spend excessive time helping me. They also worried that I could not be left alone at Korupun lest I fall and hurt myself without anyone to care for me, so I would need "sitters," potentially them. This wasn't just how I read attitudes; ExCom had heard and seen the resentment too and talked to me about it—even appointing someone to whom I could go for counsel during times I felt overwhelmed by it all.

Missionaries are imperfect, rescued sinners. One of Satan's best tools to ruin God's work in isolated situations is the old divide-and-conquer strategy. I, too, am a rescued sinner. At first, I was both deeply hurt and insulted. The situation brought back to my mind times when, as a youngster, I had to steel myself against the thinking of people who thought that since I was physically handicapped, I was subpar in every way. Those memories hurt. I reacted with cool, defensive distance. When I began to ask the Lord to deal with the other people's attitudes, he didn't answer me as I expected.

God's still voice in my heart showed me that my attitudes were comparable to theirs and just as sinful.

Seeing that, I asked the Lord to help me overcome my own wrong attitudes. He did. With relief and freedom in my spirit, I purposely began to act kindly, and as I did, our relationship improved toward acceptance of each other. Not right away—part of it took some years—but it came.

Finally, almost six months after my visit to Korupun, I was in a plane flying east of Wamena toward Korupun to stay. That one flight was a microcosm of all my years of eastern highlands flying.

As we passed over Wamena and left the Baliem Valley, in a mere ten minutes we entered clouds. The pilot, Dave, began to dip his wings and craned his neck to get a better view. I began to feel uneasy when he said under his breath, "Ninia ought to be down there somewhere." (This was before GPS devices.) Then he found it, and satisfied we were on the right course, we continued.

In another few minutes, we were over Korupun, but so were clouds. We circled several times looking for a way down. Through one hole in the clouds, I caught a glimpse of the top end of the airstrip and the aluminum roof of my house, but that hole was neither big enough nor in the right place for us. We couldn't make it in and turned back the way we had come. "I'll unload you at Ninia," Dave said. That sounded good to me; I had not yet been to Ninia.

When we got over Ninia Valley, it was clear. Clouds encircled it, but none were on the approach path or the airstrip. We circled and lowered altitude to line up for the landing. On final approach, we came what seemed (to me) close to touching the mountain with the right wing and then made a sharp turn to line up with the strip. At that point, we began bouncing violently, and Dave pulled out, climbing to gain altitude again. "Can't make it. Too windy," he said. I didn't need to be persuaded. We went back to Wamena.

The next morning, flying weather was good, and I made it to Korupun without a hitch. I was back—and back to stay.

Paul Kline and Bruce McLeay were still working on my house, so I lived in the big house with the two couples. "Your job is to learn as much Kimyal as you can these three months before we leave," Kathryn Kline said. "Work at just that. I will do the cooking, cleaning, and everything else, with Kimyal help."

All I had for language materials were some vocabulary cards Phil Masters had made and filed in a box before he died and a short grammar description of a related dialect. With those and the book, *Language Acquisition Made Practical*, I made my own language exercises. I had a battery-operated tape recorder and showed a young girl named Dayun how to speak into a microphone so I could record her saying phrases for me to practice. Dayun had been chosen to be my language helper because of her broad understanding of her language—something unusual for someone only about age twelve.

In the afternoons, I took my new expressions out on the trails and practiced them with everyone I met. Or I should say, all who came running for some entertainment as soon as they saw me outside—and that was virtually everyone around. They laughed with pleasure and amusement at my attempts at Kimyal. So did I.

Here I was, with more language study. Now a different language, and I was both the student and the instructor. The ultimate purpose of it all is what spurred me on at my desk and outside practicing each day. That purpose was to eventually put God's Word into the hands of the Kimyal people in their language. God's Word—to speak to Kimyal hearts and show them their need for him and to provide spiritual food for the new Christian Kimyals who yearned for the "big words from Sky Father." What scattered Bible verses Phil Masters and Paul Kline had given them, they repeated over and over in church or during short daily gatherings in villages so they could memorize the words.

But the job wasn't merely Scripture translation. To do that work, I had to first analyze the language: its sound system, grammar, and story structure. I also needed, as much as is possible for an outsider, to learn Kimyal culture well enough to begin to see the world as they do so the translation would be transferable to their way of thinking.

How will I ever do that? Just one day at a time, Elinor. One day at a time.

Chapter 34
MORE FIRSTS

By the fourth week of intense language study, I discovered that the materials I had—which was everything available—did not cover all aspects of what I heard as I tried to converse. I heard tone, but was it significant? Why were those infixes inserted between a verb root and a suffix not explained in the written material? So many questions. When I asked the Klines about those issues, not being linguistically trained, they said, "We don't know. You'll have to figure it out yourself." I decided to concentrate on what they did know while they were there to help me and leave my questions for another time.

Kimyal is a fascinating, complicated language. For instance, I learned that there are more than fifteen ways to say "this" or "that." Your geographic situation determines your choice. Is it below you, at the same level, or above you? Is there a river or other barrier between you and it? How far away from you is it—relatively near, not so near, or far? Can you see it? "That over there beyond the river and on the same level as where I am standing" is just one word. Also, their base-27 counting system was a challenge.

A welcome break came at the end of that first month of study. The local church prepared a big feast to celebrate a group baptism. A feast meant the death of many of their pigs. Pigs are their currency; they kill pigs only for something very significant. A baptism ranks as a feast-worthy occasion.

First, they lined big pits in the ground with banana leaves and fire-heated rocks. Then they cooked pigs and vegetables together in the pits. Sweet potatoes and sweet potato leaves, taro roots, other local edible leaves, stalks, and what in Indonesian is "sayur lilin," "candle vegetable." Its scientific name is *Setaria Palmifolia*. It does not exist in North America, so it was new to me. I fell in love with it. All the vegetables were in the bottom of the pits. Chickens and butchered pigs plus the sausages made from blood-and-fat stuffed pig intestines went on top so the fat would run down over the vegetables as everything cooked. It was all covered with banana leaves and soil and left to cook until afternoon.

As steam rose from the pits, we joined the Kimyals for the baptism and outdoor worship service.

Men made a muddy pool by damming up part of the creek that ran beside my house site. Everyone sat on the steep bank that sloped down to the pond. Following local custom, all of us Western gals sat in the women's section. The meeting started with their version of "I Have Decided to Follow Jesus." It was barely recognizable.

That's good. They are singing their way.

The other songs were in their antiphonal style and composition. They had asked Paul to preach, and then the people who would be baptized filed down to the edge of the pool. Certain ones told the crowd why they wanted to do this. Kathryn translated parts for me. Their stories showed that God had indeed changed their lives. Women who felt hope, men who quit beating their wives, and other stories. After those accounts, Kimyal elders and Dani missionaries went into the water in groups of threes and baptized four or five apiece before they switched with other elders and Dani evangelists.

After the baptism, we went to the airstrip for a communion service. Only baptized people took communion, and about 100 did, including some from other valleys who had come to see the baptism. For communion, they used pieces of sweet potatoes and the juice of tiny, dry, boiled wild raspberries. Everyone brought a container for the juice. Like many others, mine was a leaf folded into a funnel shape.

My first open-air Kimyal communion service. Simple and profound. I'm sure this is more pleasing to God than many elaborate services gilded with light from stained-glass windows.

At that altitude, the sun is intense. Soon the Kimyals around me began to sweat, and their short curly black hair started to glisten. Babies fussed, and young children squirmed or wandered about. As one mother tended her baby, she picked up the pile of leaves upon which he had done his business, wiped him with another handful of leaves, then carried the leaves to toss them into some tall grass. Then she returned to her spot without a care. And we Westerners think we invented disposable diapers?

Midmorning we went to the feast site. I perched on a large rock among other women next to one of the pits. I sat four feet higher than it was. I could feel the heat and smell the steam as it pushed through the mounded grass, leaves, and dirt. All over the hill, nearly 1,500 people sat on boulders, grass, or the ground with their backs against boulders. One of the Korupun leaders stood on a high flat rock and hollered, "Everyone be quiet and close your eyes." I couldn't hear his prayer, but I knew when he had finished, as a rumble of "amens" reached my ears.

Before they opened the dirt ovens, appointed men passed around raw food—sugar cane and what the Kimyals call yowen and kaben nuts. These nuts are delicious, moist, and sort of coconut flavored. They come from two sub-species of pandanus that grow only in the high mountains of Papua. The one-and-a-half-inch nut, thinner than a pencil, has a fibrous, woody substance on the outside that you crack with your teeth to expose the crunchy flesh of the core. The nuts lie side by side inside a ball the size and shape of a basketball. The men had split the balls in two to access the nuts.

Since it was nut season, there were ten piles of those half-basketballs, each pile five feet tall. One of the food distributors brought me a two-hand cupped amount of already shelled nuts. Yes, the nuts had been between someone's teeth. Excellent—that saved any wear on my teeth! Yum. Everyone around me got unshelled nuts. Soon cracking and popping sounds filled the air. As much as I love yuwen and kaben nuts, the Kimyals are crazy about them.

I alternately sucked sugar cane and ate nuts while men opened the pits. First, they removed the dirt on top, then lifted off the leaves that covered the first layer of food. In this pit, yellow beans and candle vegetables were first. Under those vegetables was a layer of charred banana leaves that covered the first level of hot rocks. A man took a small pole, bent it in half, and used the resulting giant-size pincher to lift the hot rocks off the vegetables. Others, with lightning speed, picked up those dangerously hot objects with their bare hands and, with perfect accuracy, threw them out of the way. Removing the hot rocks revealed another layer of banana leaves and under them, sweet potatoes, taro, chayote (a common squash in Latin America the size and shape of a pear), sweet potato greens, and other vegetables. More similar layers filled the pit. This pit didn't have any meat, but one of the distributors gave me succulent chicken and pig from another oven. Nothing tastes as delicious as pit-cooked, fat-basted, vegetable flavor-enhanced food.

I made it back home with only one mishap on the uneven, rocky, and sometimes steep trail. A kind Kimyal, trying to help me down a steep part, pulled my hand before my feet were ready to move.

This isn't working. I need to work harder to balance with this "help" than I would by myself. But what about the trails on the mountainsides? I can't walk those tiny paths. The Kimyals are too small, and the trails are too steep for me to ride shoulders as I did in Dani territory.

My mission agency's Field Executive Committee had approved a special project for me to get a mule to use on the trails if I thought that would work.

These trails look only wide enough for a goat. Besides, I haven't heard of any mules anywhere on the island.

What could the solution be? *I've got to figure out a way.* I wrote to family and friends: "Please pray I'll find the right Mountain Transport System."

Chapter 35

A HOUSE OF MY OWN

A few weeks later, I had a "break" in the Baliem Valley as the VBS teacher of six four- and five-year-olds during another mission agency's annual conference. The change was refreshment that I needed for the busy time ahead.

When I got back to Korupun, everyone focused on getting my house finished enough for me to move in by the time Paul and Kathryn Kline would leave—in just a little over a week. I would have to hire Kimyals to help me paint, varnish, and more. Judy McLeay had developed severe morning sickness, so the McLeays flew out on a personal medical emergency flight. Only Paul Kline remained to work on my house.

I knew that after the Klines moved back to Karubaga, and before the McLeays returned, I would be on my own at Korupun. What a good incentive for language study! I not only settled back into that but also took time to sew curtains for my house on my treadle sewing machine. My first seams were anything but straight. I wasn't used to using hands and feet all at once!

When I moved into my house, the decor was boxes and piles. Even so, the day before the Klines left, I cooked for them so they had time to pack the remainder of their things for their early morning flight to Karubaga where they would continue their former work.

Flights into Korupun were always first on the plane's schedule for that day, before fog or variable wind closed the strip. Early morning at our 6,000 feet elevation could be frigid. The morning the Klines left, it was. The night before, I dreamed that it had snowed, and I'm sure there was snow on Mt. Juliana that morning; the wind coming down from that direction was so cold it made my windward ear ache. I looked around at the mostly naked Kimyals hugging themselves and shivering as they also stood beside the airstrip to say goodbye to Paul and Kathryn.

When the plane lifted off and turned out of the valley, I was on my own. The Klines were gone, and the McLeays were not yet back from the south coast mission hospital. There was a lot of work to do in my house and yard. I paid a young man for a few small bundles of firewood with a sweater and men's shorts that had come in a package sent from Chattaroy. Dayun, my twelve-year-old language helper, came to help me in the kitchen, and I showed her how to wash dishes. Outside, I instructed some young men on how I wanted my garden plots built and where. Of course, I was "only a woman" and therefore not highly intelligent, so they were sure what they had in mind was better than what I, with limited language and lots of gestures, said to do. However, because I was the payer for the work, they finally complied.

That same afternoon I heard an airplane overhead.

Planes don't come in the afternoon! Even to go overhead to Langda (the only place Korupun was on the way to). There was always wind in the afternoon.

This plane dipped its wings and revved its engine: a signal to open the radio for a message. When I did, I heard, "Korupun, Mike Charlie Foxtrot," then the radio signal was so broken up that only on the fourth try did I understand that he was asking, "Is there wind?"

"Only a bit of a breeze," I answered. As the plane approached the strip, my heart lurched as I felt some gusts. It wobbled a bit in the air but landed safely. As I walked to the top of the strip, I heard the Kimyals exclaim, "It's Bruce and Judy!"

No, I thought. *MAF wouldn't try to bring them from Senggo at this time of day. They're scheduled to come in tomorrow morning.*

By the time I got to the top of the airstrip, Bruce and Judy had climbed out of the plane and were quickly removing their things. The weather was closing fast, so Glen, the pilot, stayed in the airplane. As soon as the baggage door shut, Glen was on his way down the strip and into the air. Judy said, "Oh! Let me sit down and calm down. That weather up there was horrible. I don't see how he made it." It was good to see, though, that Judy seemed fully recovered from her morning sickness. Knowing that fact, and because it fit their flight schedule better, MAF had brought the McLeays in a day early.

The plane left, and I got back to the small class where I was teaching a few Kimyals the basics of the Indonesian language and money system. That class gave them a head start on learning skills to meet the general Indonesian culture that would soon come into their world. It would enable the Kimyal people to spot outsiders who would try to cheat them. At the same time, it helped me to expand my use of Kimyal.

Back at my house, I started my kitchen fire, heated a kettle of water to wash my hair, then cooked and ate my simple lunch-like supper. That done, I lit my pressure lamp, put a box of letter-writing things on my dining table, and sat down to write.

The day had been a revelation—I would never be able to describe a "typical" day. I could set up plans and schedules, but unexpected changes were the only constant.

Chapter 36

PRAYER, VIOLENCE, AND DEMONISM

First bouts of malaria, first earthquakes, first airplane accidents during my time in Papua, first houseguests in my own home—all happened while I was trying to learn Kimyal language and culture.

And there came a good first:

I tried to force the few sentences to run through my mind once more. I was on my low camp stool surrounded by Kimyal women. Only their grass skirts were between them and the bare floor of the building used for both church and school. It was the weekly afternoon prayer meeting. Across the room, men also squatted on the floor and listened as the leader called out prayer requests. All week long, I had prepared for this. Always before I had prayed in Indonesian, but this was going to be my first public attempt to pray in Kimyal.

"Lord," I pleaded silently, "please have him ask me to pray for a village. If he gives me anything else, I'm sunk."

The elder called a name. "You pray for our potato crops," he said. To another, "Pray for the Dani missionaries." To still another, "Pray for the pale people learning our words." Then, "Eleenod. You pray for Segeddam village."

My heart pounded as I nodded in agreement. *Come on,* I scolded myself. *Don't get nervous. You'll forget and foul the whole thing up.*

Suddenly, the request time finished, and someone began to pray. I waited for my chance, and when there was a pause, I began, "Eim Ayong, Na'Neyong . . ." (Sky Father, my Father . . .) and carefully went through the seven short sentences of my first Kimyal prayer. My heart raced faster with each one. When I finished, the crowd verbally echoed my "Amen" in a manner usually reserved for the closing prayer. Were they "amening" what I said, or the accomplishment of my having said it? Maybe it was a milestone for them too—the first time when we, with mutual understanding, joined in talking to our heavenly Father, "Sky Father."

A few weeks after my first Kimyal prayer, a man came running from the Duram Valley, which was over a ridge and across a river from Korupun. "Bruce must come quick. Now! A Yali man from Solu Valley struck a Duram man in the head with a stone adze. The man's spirit is small inside him." I learned that meant he was unconscious, and they didn't expect him to live.

Bruce left immediately, at noon, hoping the man would not die before he could get there and arrange for the man to be brought to Korupun. Without medical help, he would die for sure, and serious fighting between tribes would likely result in more deaths. This was urgent. While Bruce was on the trail, Judy got on the radio to ask MAF to plan a possible emergency flight in the morning. We would know for sure late afternoon when Bruce got back. Bruce was a quick trekker, so it took only five hours for him to make the round trip, including bandaging the man as best he could and finding men to carry the victim to Korupun.

When Bruce returned, he told us the story. It was a dispute over a bride price. The adze-wielding man thought that he was due a refund because the girl ran away. The two men had agreed to talk it over in the morning, but in the middle of the night, the "cheated" man got up and hit the other man in the ear with his stone adze. He meant the blow to hit below the ear. If it had, the man would have died for sure. As it was, he bled a lot and was very weak but was still alive.

The carriers arrived at Korupun with the injured man an hour behind Bruce. The guilty man was also with the party, led by the same rope that tied his hands in front of him. As the Duram group neared the center of Korupun Valley, people from villages all around lined up to get a good look at both the victim and the culprit.

The next day, the patient and his helper were flown to the hospital at Karubaga. The wrongdoer remained at Korupun. He was free of constraints, though closely guarded. In three and a half days, a delegation of Yalis from Ninia arrived to bring the two sides together and come to an agreement that would satisfy both. It took a whole day of discussions among the men. Women were never included in legal negotiations, even if, as here, the outcome affected them.

The runaway wife who had sparked the attack was paid for when she was very young. When the man who bought her took her, she didn't want him and fled. Before the Yali delegation left, the man of highest rank from Ninia called for everyone to gather for a public meeting.

"Stop your practice of paying for girls as wives when they are too young to say yes or no," he urged. He had two girls up front to illustrate. One was about ten years old. "This one is too young," he said. Of the one who was about fourteen, he said, "This age is good."

———— ✿ ————

Language is rooted in culture. I couldn't learn its heart without learning its culture. Besides a chance to hear new words and grammar, local events supplied a lot of cultural insight. *I need to learn more about a Kimyal woman's life,* I told myself. I chose a woman to visit—a woman in a nearby village. These visits became my routine once or twice a week, in the afternoon after the women returned from their potato gardens.

A single larger hut stands in the middle of each Kimyal village— the men's house. Circling it are the huts of their wives. Each Kimyal wife has a separate dwelling—a round structure eight or nine feet in diameter, covered with a grass roof. Inside, the only light comes from a small doorway that is about eighteen-by-twenty-six and about fifteen inches above the ground. Even I had trouble doubling up to get in and out of those doors. There is no room to stand up inside; one must sit on the floor. Both ceiling and floor are made of small canes laid side by side and bound together. There are no windows and no smoke hole. Smoke from the fire in the middle of the house escapes by seeping through the grass roof or the small cracks between the wallboards. The fire is kept just smoldering to save on firewood. A rack above the fire holds a few days' supply of wood, keeping dry. The ceiling is sticky black from the smoke always drenching it.

A hole in the ceiling gives access to the sleeping loft that is the upper side of the ceiling reeds. That allows more room for someone to stretch out because part of the ground-level floor is a sleeping area for the wife's pigs. A woman, her daughters, and her young sons sleep with her in her hut. Her husband spends most nights with the men in the shared larger men's hut. Most often a man eats with a wife and children, though, and sometimes sleeps there too. However, he does not spend the night if his wife is nursing a child, which they do for two or three years—one of the reasons to have more than one wife.

One day I went to Dayun's village and wandered around talking to whoever would respond. They all wanted to know why I had come: did I want to pay Dayun? "No, I've come for different," I answered, which is grammatically correct in Kimyal, meaning loosely, "Nothing significant." Soon Elbusu, a friend, came from her potato gardens, so I sat in her hut while she blew up her fire and put her potatoes in the ashes to cook. And we talked—as best we could.

I realized that I never could remember Elbusu's name until I sat in her house, saw how she lived, and saw her as an individual. Those visits unmassed "the people." I began to see them as distinct persons. They were certainly of a different culture from my native land. Learning their distinctions up close made them real, with names and faces, feelings, and intelligence.

I knew in theory that demons, whom the Kimyals identified as ancestor spirits, were what controlled Kimyal culture. My first up close view of that reality came not long after the adze-to-the-head incident.

I was at my kitchen door paying my grass-cutting boys with salt when loud men's voices sprang into the scene, proclaiming to all that a delegation was descending the trail from Sela to Korupun. I looked at the side of that mountain but could hardly make them out.

Kimyal eyes must be keen! How did they happen to see the entourage? The visitors were only as distinct as a pin-dot on a piece of paper. They came down the mountain, crossed the river (not visible from my house), came to and across the airstrip and, finally, they passed in front of my house on their way to the clinic. That's when I got a good look. They carried a make-shift stretcher on which lay a man who appeared to be half wrapped in bandages. I joined the curious who went to the clinic to see what this was all about.

It was a teenage boy stoically enduring the pain of extensive burns suffered when he had sat in a fire the day before. Togwi, the Dani medical worker that the Dani church had sent to Sela in response to our request for one, had dressed the scorched skin as best he could. He gave the boy a shot of penicillin, then, after they made the stretcher, Togwi and several others started over the long steep trail to Korupun. Darkness closed in on them halfway, so they spent the night in a small village and set out again as soon as it was light. It was now 1:00 p.m., double the usual time it took to walk that trail.

The boy had not been in control when he sat on the fire. Nor was the cause an epileptic seizure. He didn't thrash around. Unable to move due to a trance, he remained on the fire until the meat of his buttocks cooked to a hard crust. Consequently, he had first-, second-, and third-degree burns on his buttocks, private parts, thighs, and down past his knees.

By the time I saw the boy, Bruce was already on the radio to Dr. Liz at Soba, Dr. Donaldson at Karubaga, and MAF at Wamena to arrange an emergency medical flight. Fog had already closed down our airstrip for that day, but hopefully the next morning a plane could come and take the boy and an attendant to Soba first and see if Dr. Liz, with her limited facilities, could help him.

Liz examined the boy, but he needed more help, and for longer, than she could give. Liz sent the injured boy to Karubaga. She also said that the Dani medical orderly, Togwi, and Bruce had done all the right things for him.

In a letter home, I wrote,

> I know that many people at home would poo-poo the idea of spirit control, but if they were here, it wouldn't be long before they changed their tune. The Kimyals know that demonic powers are real, and we know it too. We have seen too much evidence, backed up by Scripture, not to believe. Yet people who have never been here say, "They are happy as they are; leave them alone." I think that boy is evidence enough to show that when Satan controls people, he does not have their happiness in mind. Even if demonic sources did not cause the boy's burns—let's say it was just a "natural occurrence"—if we had not been here, that boy would have died an agonizing, pain-ridden, infection-filled death. Even now he may die, but if so, it won't be as horrible a death. And some say we should not have come?

Over the years I would encounter more experiences with demon activity, including times I was the target.

Chapter 37
GRIEF, COMFORT, AND GOALS

Despite everything I learned in those first months, some days I felt overwhelmed by the mountain of what I still did not know about the Kimyal language and culture.

One day, as I visited one of the Dani wives, she said I had a weak or soft (same word) head. In their culture, that was not an insult. It meant that it was not hard to get knowledge into my head—specifically, learning Kimyal. I took the compliment with gratefulness but with inward skepticism. After all, the fact that she made such a statement said that my speech drew attention to the fact that I was learning. That very day I made a goof that contradicted the earlier praise. A little boy on my kitchen porch had a runny nose, so I told him to "yublom" it. Songmag (Smelly Water), working in my kitchen, heard that and laughed. I had told the boy to cook it, instead of "lublom," wipe it.

As I learned Kimyal, I realized that several people had names that meant something. Isinggom, for example, means No Eyes, but in fact, she had pretty eyes. Elbusu, whom I mentioned before, means His/Her Dust, His/Her Steam, or His/Her Wind. There were more. The significance wasn't always obvious. I knew there must be a story behind the names, and I determined to stay alert for clues of those stories.

Other discoveries were very complicated. I began writing explanations for whoever might follow me in learning Kimyal. Before long I had five typed pages that were hardly a start on the verb system. I had counted, so far, 444 possible verb forms for a single verb and knew there were more I hadn't figured out. The quest revved me up when, after long hours of study, I would say out loud, "Hey, that's how it works. Wow, that's neat!"

I had accomplished my first public Kimyal prayer by setting a goal to do that by a specific date. It had been a push, but I did it. Now I set a goal to do my first preliminary Scripture translation in six months. Could I? I would try and find out. The young Kimyal church desperately needed it.

As I concentrated on language study, my mind often roamed to thoughts of my dad. He had written me a "Dear Daughter" (his love name for me) letter to tell me he had cancer and was at peace with whatever God had for him. The most recent letter from Mom said that surgery had been successful; Dad was doing well.

The next week, Bruce sent a note to me from his house: "The Missions Fellowship has a cable to read to you. Come to the radio." I did and heard the cablegram. My sweet daddy was in heaven. The funeral was that very day. The cable had taken three days to get to Jayapura. I was acutely aware of the long miles and days between loved ones and me.

It seemed that nothing else mattered. Why was everything going on as usual? Didn't the world know Dad was dead? My dad, who had given all he had to make possible whatever I wanted to do, even through my disrespectful teenage stage. Such love! Without it, nothing would ever be the same.

Even years later as I write this, I cry. I also remember that not being able to study or do anything, two days later I was outside walking around when a small boy stopped and faced me on the path.

"I hear your father died," he said.

"Yes, he did."

"I'm sorry. I will pray for you."

Those words from a small Kimyal boy remain a great comfort.

Christmas was in a couple of weeks, and I flew west and a bit south to be with some friends at Mapnduma who worked with the Nduga tribe. My grief was still raw, but being with friends doing fun activities helped. I saw some things I could not have imagined—like an angel with his halo through the septum hole in his nose where he used to hold a boar's fang.

The Mapnduma church put on a Christmas pageant. Two men played angel parts. They had gotten some stiff tinsel ropes from one of the missionaries. These they used as halos—one red and one blue. The blue-haloed man thought he would improve on the white people's pictures of angels. A small generator outside lit just one light bulb in the church, so the first couple of times that this angel came in, I thought I didn't see it right. But the third time, I took a good look, and sure enough—there it was, a "halo" proudly around the head and through the nose. After all, to properly gussy up, the halo goes through your nose, not precariously perched on your forehead.

Herod put on a good show too. When the wise men came to him, he sat on his throne as two men at his side waved feather dusters. They dusted Herod from head to foot and kept it up for the whole ten-plus minutes he was on stage. When the wise men asked Herod about the new King of the Jews, he sat silently for a moment, then sprang up with a "BAAAAAH!" That made us all jump. Well, he was a bad guy, wasn't he? The actors wanted to leave no doubt.

Another thing not left in doubt was how Herod died. After he had all the boy babies killed, he got a terrible stomachache and writhed in pain before they carried him out dead.

I couldn't understand the Nduga language, but the graphic play was easy to follow. Delightful. All planned, practiced, and put on by the Ndugas. The missionaries just supplied the requested props.

Another fun time was our Mountain Transportation brain-storm session. We planned a two-hour hike to a picnic spot and wanted a good way to get me there. We held a brainstorming session the night before.

I told my friends about my quest for a workable way of getting around the trails, and when I mentioned a mule, my hostess, Elfrieda, registered mouth-open, eyes-wide shock and horror. Someone got a pad of paper and a pencil and started sketching with input from

RUNNING ON BROKEN LEGS

us all. We came up with a simple carrying device of two poles held at the width of a man's shoulders by a cross-stick lashed to them, a net bag, and some vine to tie it all together. We would fold the net bag in half and bind it to the poles to hang a foot or so below the poles. Then we would place a board at the bottom for me to sit on.

The next morning a crowd gathered in front of the kitchen door. In the middle were two poles, a net bag, and a short piece of board. We started to manufacture what we had drawn. Soon the contraption was put together, I was in it, lifted, the poles put on shoulders, and we were ready to. Go we did, with whoops and hollers. My carriers went at a fast clip; Elfrieda was the only one who could keep up. Finally, someone said, "Elfrieda! Tell them to slow down!" We, our carriers, and those who came along to see what those silly white women were doing wound our way along the trail. The green near mountains and far blue ones, the sight and sound of running water, the fresh breeze, chatter in a language I didn't know, the bright sky pocked by random white clouds—it all made the trek seem almost unreal. Unreal except for steep places where I had to hang on tight. But it worked. I knew that with such a conveyance I could go anywhere. No wonder God made me small and light.

Chapter 38
SHAKEN

When I got back to Korupun, I oversaw the making of a pole Mountain Transport System (MTS) there. With it, I got to villages farther away from the airstrip and could see more of primal everyday Kimyal life, hear the language, and glimpse some of the darkness within the culture. One day that vile side spread from one village and touched the whole valley.

That day, a boy of about nine began to scratch some things on the outside of a men's hut. The head man, "Part Eyes," heard it, went outside, and asked who did it. The guilty boy pointed at another boy. Part Eyes told him to quit. The boy responded, "Eat feces." Children regularly talked back to adults, so that wasn't unusual, but Part Eyes was already angry at that boy for stealing a bird out of his trap and eating it. He flew into a rage, beat the boy, tied a rope around his feet, and suspended him head down in a toilet hole that had water in the bottom. The boy's hands were free, so he managed to claw his way up and out. When he got up, he sang a defiant song at Part Eyes. That further enraged Part Eyes. The village chief said, "Don't you know God's words? That's enough! Give the boy to me."

Part Eyes replied, "So are you going to pay me a pig?" The Kimyals usually settled disputes with pig payments. The chief couldn't do that right then, which left him powerless to do anything. So Part Eyes tied the boy's hands, put him back down the hole, and put a rock over his feet. The boy couldn't get out, let alone lift his head above the water. He drowned before he was pulled up again.

That night, imaginary scenes of that poor little boy's agony kept playing in my mind.

Traditionally, this murder would have resulted in war and revenge killings on both sides that could have gone on for years. However, both the gospel and government influence was enough to bring clan chiefs together to discuss how to involve a government agent who would decide a penalty. They asked Bruce to contact, by radio, the correct government person at Wamena. Bruce did, MAF flew that agent to Korupun, he held a trial, levied fines of pig payments, and sentenced Part Eyes to jail in Wamena.

This time war didn't break out, but it showed me how explosive the Kimyals were. That, mixed with the darkness of their slavery to the wicked ways demanded by the ancestor spirits, is lethal. Only the knowledge of Jesus could bring light and make this deep darkness retreat. I knew that the peaceful-looking setting of the mountain-enclosed Korupun Valley hid emotional volcanoes that could erupt at any minute.

Even so, the beauty didn't escape me. Sharp cliffs rose above steep mountainsides dotted by garden mounds. Mountainsides stood so steep that when a group carried someone to the clinic and said, "He fell out of his garden," it was true. The sounding-board cliffs supplied the never-ending background roar of the Disul River as it dropped one thousand feet in its one-mile run through the valley. Several waterfalls on the rim of the valley added their voices to the water-over-rock music. The composition was worthy of sleep therapy recordings.

Then, one night, the mountains betrayed us. At about 4:30 a.m., I woke to my bed shaking so hard I had to hang on to my mattress so I wouldn't be shaken off. In the darkness, I heard cans crashing off shelves in my pantry and kitchen and vases and books landing on the floor. Even the kerosene lamp by my bed fell off its stand and shattered.

When the shaking stopped, I grabbed a flashlight and bathrobe, put on my shoes, and walked through the house to assess the damage. When I reached the kitchen, I heard a roar that sounded like a thousand rifles fired at once. Or like the mountains collapsing. The earthquake had started landslides all around us. Their sharp rumble echoed and re-echoed in the still night air.

I opened the kitchen door and stepped out on the porch, straining my eyes toward the roar, but saw nothing in the blackness.

I knew Bruce and Judy had guests. Everyone would be out of their house, and they would send someone to check on me. Soon I saw a small beam from a flashlight amble in a slow molasses style I recognized. It was their guest, a missionary from the north slope of the mountains, Johnny.

"Ya' aw right?" he asked in his slow southern drawl.

"Yes, I'm fine," I chuckled. I noticed that Johnny had taken the time to get fully dressed before going outside the McLeay's house. We chatted for a while and futilely tried to see what was happening in the direction of the loudest-sounding landslides on the cliffs surrounding Korupun Valley. Johnny said, "Shore wish I could see what's goin' awn up thar."

It was so cold I was shivering in my quilted bathrobe, so I said I had better get back inside. Earth tremors kept coming, but they didn't seem too bad, so Johnny left. I went back to my bed and crawled inside its warmth. Sleep was brief if at all, and though it was my usual Saturday sleep-in day, I got up early.

Tremors and small landslides continued all day. I happened to be watching when the soil on one cliff face broke loose and kept falling in a great rumble that turned into a mild grumble that turned into a splashing sound as it changed from dirt to mud to water. The waterfall it created is still there and runs continuously.

This is like watching creation happen.

Though the earth tremors were disconcerting, I felt safe enough, but Bruce and Judy were afraid the mountain behind my house would slide down on top of me. That night they set up a bed for me in their kitchen, and they slept in the living room. They left a pressure lamp on all night so we could see to evacuate if we needed to. I slept well, considering all the tremors, but Judy didn't—understandable for a mom of a small baby.

Bruce and Judy decided that she and I should leave Korupun the next morning. However, when Bruce contacted MAF, they said they had no plane available to take us out. All planes were flying food, injured people, and government personnel around the worst-hit areas. The next day, though, they could come and get us. Bruce began to reconsider. I yearned to stay, but I could see that Judy needed to get away, so I said I did too. Bruce confirmed the flight for Judy, the baby, and me to leave.

Our plane landed first at Ninia, where we picked up Sheila, the nurse. She also felt the need to get away from all the shaking. Judy and baby went to Wamena, then to Sentani. Sheila and I went to Karubaga.

I hated being away from Korupun. *What does this say to the Kimyals?* I asked myself. *They can't escape, and they need our help and reassurance. I feel like I have abandoned them.* There was no loss of life at Korupun, though some villages were abandoned, and everyone lost gardens.

Two weeks later, Bruce said I could come back if someone came with me. Sheila agreed to do that, and Bruce went to Sentani to be with Judy and the baby. Sheila and I went back to Ninia.

Not only was Korupun hit by the earthquake, but the area was also hard hit by the flu. They desperately needed the medical help Sheila could give. However, despite the desperate situation or perhaps because of it, I didn't return to Korupun right away, nor did Sheila come in. MAF more urgently needed their airplanes to go elsewhere.

The aftermath of the earthquake was worse just north of us, on the north slope of the ranges where related tribes live. A count after two weeks showed that, in those areas, 350 people were known dead and thousands unaccounted for and assumed to be sheltering in the forest. Landslides had covered entire villages with their inhabitants and destroyed 80 percent of garden areas. Fifteen thousand people faced starvation.

I heard a Voice of America report on my short-wave radio and almost laughed when they said, "Some cropland was destroyed, and a food shortage is feared." It is hard for Western countries to understand what it means when your food comes from your daily trips to your gardens. When you wake up in the morning and find those gardens gone, you go on a forced fast.

International news reports also said that people were being evacuated. They weren't. There was no place for them to go. The only solution was to find help to reestablish villages and gardens where they had been and give food relief in the meantime.

The government sent airplanes and helicopters with loads of rice to all affected areas, and Danis and other tribes contributed sweet potatoes and other crops. MAF assigned one plane and one helicopter to full-time relief flights for months. Helicopters dropped sweet potato vines as well as tubers, and the affected areas planted those vines right away, but it takes six months for sweet potato vines to produce. Besides, how fast could they build and plant gardens when they were weak from hunger and sick with flu? It's very hard work.

Circumstances and another major aftershock kept me away from Korupun for five weeks, not the planned two. Two weeks were at Ninia. While there, I joined the Yalis and missionaries for Sunday church. John Wilson translated the sermon for me. The first Sunday, the first announcement by the Yali leader was, "If we get a big shake, nobody move until we get Miss Elinor out of the building." That went straight to my heart and forever endeared them to me.

Meanwhile, all the mountainsides of the Korupun Valley were nude from the loss of vegetation. Higher up, in the worst affected areas, mountain forests were now naked brown earth. The quake had registered seven on the Richter scale and nine on the twelve-point Indonesian scale.

When I finally landed back at Korupun, it was not Sheila who was with me, but another nurse, one from the Dani area of Mamit: Margaret, and her daughter, Rebeka.

In a week or two, Margaret and Rebeka left, and the McLeays came back to Korupun. We got into a day-by-day, week-by-week routine of handling the tasks of helping the Kimyals restore their gardens and their lives. But not for long. Judy had continuing health problems that included dizziness and lethargy. They needed to go home to New Zealand to find an answer. *So how could this affect me?* I wondered.

Soon I was back to trying to balance my and the Kimyals' need for me to be at Korupun with the risk to my mental health from too much time in this still-stressful situation of trying to relieve the hungry, the ill, the grieving, and the destitute without another Westerner's company. The field ExCom said that I could not be without ex-patriot company at Korupun for more than two weeks at a time. Either I would go out or someone would come in for a while. Of course, it had to be someone who wasn't nervous about the booming and shaking still happening.

Now and then we heard what sounded like a sonic boom, but instead of originating from a jet overhead, it came from the ground beneath us, accompanied by slight vibrations. Small after-tremors were frequent too. It is an eerie feeling not knowing if you can rely on the earth to be a solid foundation. Years later I learned that the booms and vibrations were from tectonic plates adjusting against each other.

I had to adjust too. Again. Some more.

Chapter 39
JUGGLING ROLES

When the relief work was almost at an end, field leadership began to think again about discovering and planning for the spiritual needs of outlying areas near Korupun. Our field chairman visited Korupun and took a two-day helicopter survey of the whole Kimyal territory. Then he, together with the rest of ExCom, decided two things that affected my work.

One decision was a plan for work in the Sela area. Months earlier, Bruce McLeay had walked across the mountains to the upper Sela Valley, surveyed a place to build an airstrip, and brought in some Dani workers to do that. The Korupun and Sela Valley systems marked the two main divisions of the Kimyal tribe. Bruce wanted to offer consistent gospel teaching in Sela and to locate there eventually. However, the McLeays were gone for an undetermined time, and I could not take over the supervision of making the airstrip even if I went in by helicopter, not by trail. ExCom decided to appoint a Dani or Yali-speaking missionary to do that. I would go along in the helicopter and visit villages in the sub-valleys further out.

The other decision concerned language analysis. The Korupun and Sela Valley system areas of the Kimyal tribe had dialects that they could mutually easily understand. Even I caught on quickly to the word exchanges. ExCom wanted me to do a language survey of the more distant villages. Some dialects, we suspected, especially in the Sela Valley system, might be closer to a language southeast of Korupun Kimyal. Getting dialect data was essential for strategies of getting the gospel into those places. It would not be wise, though, in those villages that had never seen white skin, for me to drop in without a male missionary—other than the heli pilot. The village men might not be friendly. We planned for who would go with me on those visits, and when.

In the meantime, small earth tremors continued as I settled into my new routine of handling all station matters and duties—teaching, bookkeeping, medical clinic, consultations that came to my door, arranging flights for supplies, handling the little weekly trade store we had where the Kimyals could spend their wages for work or profits from selling me vegetables, and doing the unexpected.

Around me, tense faces registered stress from the frequent shaking of the ground.

During one of my weeks without Western culture company, I decided to relieve the local people's anxiety with something fun. An open house. It was normal for them to pop in by ones or twos, but that day for two hours I opened both doors wide and invited everyone to stream in and out as they pleased. Eyes glinted with excitement. My house, in contrast to their tiny huts that one couldn't even stand up in, seemed like a palace. Everything was a pure marvel to them. One little boy, who had been through before, appointed himself the tour guide. Pointing to my bathroom mirror, he said, "This is for Elinod to see if her face is dirty, and if it is (pointing to my sink), she washes it there. And *this* (pointing to my bar of Camay), is her soap!" The cheap bars of yellow trade soap were a treasure to them. My soap was a spectacle.

That fun interlude over, I again put my mind to the needs of the emerging church.

Bruce had started a meeting each Friday with a small group of elders. He taught them a Bible story and its core concept so they would have fresh, solid teaching for their churches on Sunday morning. Now that Bruce was gone, I filled that role with the church leaders.

Most Bible stories were still unknown to the Kimyals, but I thought, *my goal is to one day translate the Kimyal Bible. Why not take baby steps now and translate, rather than paraphrase the story?*

I chose Matthew 2:1–12. I had only seventeen months of Kimyal study behind me. Those twelve verses and simple lesson questions took me two whole days—one of them into the night—to translate, check, type ditto machine masters, and run them off. Even though a team of four Kimyal men and I took two and a half hours to go over my work word by word before I typed it, my translation lacked a lot, and I knew it.

I felt a responsibility to be as careful, careful, careful as possible to avoid mistakes that might lead to critical misunderstanding of Scripture truth. During the process, I learned a new Kimyal word: *Help*. A word I had tried to find for a long time.

Soon, armed with my fresh-off-the-press verses and questions, I entered the school building. A few of the men prayed, and it was time for me to teach. As I read the Scripture passage through twice, then taught from it, I was amazed at what I heard rolling off my tongue. I didn't usually speak Kimyal that well. *Thank you, Lord! I'm so encouraged.*

When the meeting was over, I headed up the path toward home to relax over a soothing cup of coffee. However, some elders followed me, and before I entered my house, they said what I had heard many times: "Quickly finish God's Word for us. We hunger for it as we do for our sweet potatoes. Our spirits are heavy. Because we don't have God's Word, we don't know what God wants us to do. We want to go to bed sleeping with it. You have many books with God's Word. When you sleep, it is there with you. We don't have even one book."

My heart ached. So much had kept me from trying translation until now. The earthquake and resulting relief flights and ground-to-air radio traffic, my frequent trips out and other people coming in, no other missionary on station to respond to the Kimyals' questions and ideas—a myriad of things got in the way. Besides, my Kimyal was not yet good enough for "real" translation.

My Kimyal is still very basic, but I did an OK-for-now job. With enough time and sweat, I can do it again. I wrote in simple language, but to the best of my knowledge, it is truthful. I must give them what I can.

The time necessary to do that would become even more scarce.

Chapter 40

MOUNTAIN CLIMBING

It is hard to maintain a sloping airstrip at 5,800 feet elevation in mountains where it rains over 200 inches in a year and where it is impossible to bring in tractors, trucks, bulldozers, or anything motorized. But when the only other way to get people and supplies in and out is a narrow, steep trail that is days to the nearest other airstrip, you must take care of yours. That means time—lots of it.

I wanted to spend more time on language so that I could do better Bible translation, but our airstrip had become slimy with moss. That did not please the pilots who would land and come sliding sideways up the strip, hoping they would stop before the big rocks at the top. Slimy moss also made takeoff more exciting. MAF's head of safety issues said, "Sorry, but I have to put a load restriction on the Korupun airstrip until the moss is gone and gravel is on." That meant fewer people and pounds of baggage per load, right at a time when more than the usual number of Dani evangelists and Kimyal medical patients needed to come and go—not to speak of my and my guest's flights every two weeks.

I became the airstrip maintenance employer and supervisor. Without tractors or bulldozers, the surface of the strip was scraped down to the dirt with shovels. Gravel for the top came in net bags from the river fifteen minutes away. How long does it take to resurface a 1,250-foot-long airstrip? Weeks. But that repair was minor. It would keep the strip minimally open for a short time, but then we needed to crown it and remove the worst "bounder" bump that had always been at the bottom. MAF said it was time for it to go.

The grades of 9 to 15 to 13 percent from the bottom to the top of the strip were enough of a challenge for a landing airplane without adding in the bumps. Field leadership assigned two male colleagues to come in and handle bump removal. It was way out of my league!

While all that was going on and after my nurse friend Sheila came from Ninia to spend a few weeks with me, one day a church leader from the Duram Valley came.

"Come to our baptism next Sunday." No one worked on the airstrip on weekends.

In the straightforward Kimyal way of speaking, an invitation sounded more like a command. I knew that the trek would take two hours, then there would be the time taken for a church service, baptisms, and pit-cooked food to celebrate. I had never gone that many miles away, let alone over a footpath between two valleys. It would be a lot of mountain climbing and descending, river crossings, being jostled, and hanging on tight to my carrier poles.

"Na'e. Besarob noong. Od bununa'" (Thank you. Very good. I will go), I said, thinking, *Sounds grueling but fun.* Sheila said she would rather stay and keep the fire going and have things clean for my return.

So that Sunday, eight carriers and I set off. At the start, one man carried each end of the poles. As they got tired, others would take their place. When the trail seemed to go straight down or disappear, more hands grabbed the now vertical poles as I stood on the front cross-piece to keep from being dumped out. We picked our way down landslides littered with huge boulders or made our way down the face of a rock that was running with water. In those places, there were little outcroppings of rocks just wide enough to plant one foot—something only bare feet with strong toes could grip. Our immediate destination was a spot above the gorge where a long, suspension bridge spanned the white-water river. It tilted at a forty-five-degree angle sideways, making me adjust to a compensating tilt on my carrier seat. When we got across, we started just as steep a climb as we had come down. At that point, elders from the Duram church joined us to take over for my tired carriers.

When we reached the village, elation, festivity, gifts of food, and warm sunshine revived us all. About 150 people were in the church perched on the top of a ridge. Boulders littered the whole village, but the people had taken advantage of that resource to build some terraces on the uneven ground. I couldn't walk around much because the people crowded so closely, I could hardly breathe. I was to learn that in Kimyal culture, crowding around a guest also shows welcome. That welcome was evident when they gave me gifts of one chicken and three net bags to show how glad they were that I had come.

Church service, baptisms, and eating finished, we headed back to Korupun. Despite the energy they had spent on the way to Duram, my carriers were light-hearted and seemed to fly as we headed back down to that wonky bridge. They chanted and sang as we went, so I started singing too. Redd Harper's song, "You laid your hand, mighty Lord, on the range . . . Lord, you poured forth the fountains, Raised up the mountains, O Lord, keep your mighty hand on me," seemed to fit the scene. My carriers wanted to know the words, so I translated it on the fly, best as I could.

"When we get back to Korupun, write it down, and teach it to us."

"OK," I said, though I knew that by the time they Kimyalized the tune it would hardly be recognizable. *I will love it, but would Redd Harper?*

"Welcome home!" When we arrived back, Shiela had water already hot on the stove for a bath. Delicious aromas from the meal she had ready filled the kitchen, and her happy presence topped it all off. I could relax and rest—at least for now.

Over the next months, other missionary friends came with the double purpose of companionship for me and to help with the work.

In a way, that trip to Duram was a parable of all the other mountains I had to climb but could not without a lot of help.

Vertical mountains, treacherously steep paths, and scary uphill bridges. One mountain was trying, by letters, to raise enough money to buy land and build a school for the children at Korupun. Also, field leadership had asked me to write an article for the mission magazine, part of a field orientation paper, and an essay about the Kimyal language. All in addition to my daily duties. I was exhausted trying to climb those mountains.

Then the McLeays sent word from New Zealand: "Judy's health requires that we delay our return several months."

"Lord," I prayed, "I have eight months until home leave. If Bruce and Judy return, it may not be while I'm still here. I love the help I've had, but it means extra work to cook, clean, and organize. I'm tired physically and emotionally. About to fall apart. Having solid hope of long-term teammates would help me hold on. Would you please arrange for someone else to come?"

Chapter 41

AMATEUR TROPICAL MEDICINE

My red-headed friend Charlotte, whom I met at my Indonesian language course, was also alone working with a tribe, with just an occasional representative coming in to see how she was. That tribe lived down in the hot north lowland jungle. Charlotte's mission organization required her, too, to have company regularly. She had been with me at Korupun, and we left from there together for her outpost, Wedi.

On the way, we stopped off at Soba to leave a patient for Dr. Liz to treat. His case was as unusual as the way he presented himself to me.

One late afternoon a week earlier, I looked up at the trail on the side of the cliff—the trail to Sela—and saw a line of men coming down. *That's strange at this time of day,* I thought.

Among the group, a young man with a walking stick hobbled along on obviously sore feet. As he got closer, I saw that he was not from upper Sela, where we had evangelists. People from areas where the gospel hadn't yet reached had a different look about them—a guarded, suspicious expression. He had that look. He also appeared scared but trying to be brave, curious but trying to be nonchalant. More than anything, he looked sore and tired. I guessed he was about fifteen years of age.

The men who came with the young man were a few from upper Sela villages and a couple of Dani missionaries who lived there. "We brought him for medical help," they said. This young man had hard round nobs the size of a shooter marble in clusters at his elbows and knees. On his feet, the nobs were under the skin, badly deforming his feet and making it painful to walk.

How in the world could he walk all that way over the trail?

Walking from his village to upper Sela would have been two or three days, then from Sela to Korupun was eight to ten hours by steep trail.

As bad as his feet, knees, and elbows were, I cringed at two large soft sacks of something in the skin that hung from his rectal area. Also, his eyes had a white rim in a crescent at the bottom edge of each iris. The young man's companions told me that he had frequent nosebleeds.

All I knew to do was give him an aspirin to relieve his pain, a can of fish to give him strength, and a promise to talk to a doctor in the morning.

The next day, I arranged to send him to Dr. Liz at Soba in two weeks, the soonest we could do that. The young man's friends said he had been that way for a year, so I figured two more weeks would be fine.

The young fellow had never seen an airplane up close before, only ones high above him in the sky. When our plane landed and roared up the strip, his eyes nearly bugged out as he squatted, hiding, behind the picket fence along my yard. As we walked up to the plane, he shook from head to toe. When we boarded the plane, I put him beside me in the two side-by-side middle seats. As we roared down the strip for takeoff, he leaned as close to me as his seatbelt/shoulder harness would allow and gripped my hand as if he'd never let go. Once in the air, he relaxed a bit but took only glances out of the windows. His overwhelmed mind seemed to be mush, unable to convert my Korupun dialect words into his lower Sela dialect. I tried to soothe him as best I could.

Our patient didn't react to landing as desperately as he had to takeoff. He had jumped from the Stone Age into the space age with one mighty leap.

Later, Dr. Liz operated on the young man, but only to take the lumps off his elbows and knees. She sent samples to Papua New Guinea, and when the results reported no cancer, she did what she could to relieve his feet and buttocks with more surgery. She sent some of the tissue to England, and tests revealed a very rare cholesterol deposit condition. That was astonishing considering a native diet of almost no cholesterol.

But none of that was known as Charlotte and I flew on to Wedi.

Charlotte is fun, and Wedi is like a world away from Korupun. It will be a good break for me. And fun to hear the Duvle language.

Hot and sunny every day, it was a change for sure. We were taking our baths in the river one day when some people came out of the jungle, carrying a young man of about sixteen. He had hurt his foot. Tight faces asked, "Will you take a look?"

The boy's friends' voices tumbled over each other with separate bits of the story. Charlotte pieced it together for me.

He had been chopping down a tree. As it fell, it unexpectedly uprooted and the roots or something struck the top of his left foot, or he got tangled up in them . . . it was not clear what happened, but it was a mess.

Charlotte didn't have the stomach for these things, so she left me to clean it up and see what I could do. First, I had someone bring me some warm water with a little salt in it. That would soak the dirt and dried blood off so I could see the wound and would also disinfect it a bit. There was no anesthetic in the tiny clinic. As if the pain were mine, my jaws tightened as I cleaned the foot. Some of the skin was gone, but I could peel back a great flap of skin to expose the white tendons and flesh of his toes. I tried to stitch the skin down, but it was so leather-like I couldn't get a needle through it. Besides, this was way beyond my skill. I put some butterfly band-aids on the wound, wrapped it in bandages, gave the boy a penicillin shot, and called a missionary doctor on the radio. He confirmed the need to send our patient by plane to a mission hospital. We did that the next day.

That patient spent several months away for skin grafts, healing, and therapy.

I also had to help a six-year-old girl who, three days earlier, had put her finger through the hole in the end piece of an old battery. By the time she came to us, the finger was too swollen to come out of the hole. I cut the battery piece off with a large pair of utility scissors, the only thing we could find that would work. Then I soaked the finger, bandaged it up, and gave the girl a shot of penicillin.

These may not sound like relaxing activities, but the change of surroundings and events were therapeutic, and except for medical emergencies, nothing else was my responsibility. I had a lot of time to myself. I worked on all the things my field leaders wanted me to write, plus I wrote personal letters. Making progress on those eased my mind.

Chapter 42

THE END OF THE BEGINNING

One day at Wedi I heard a radio message from ExCom: "A new couple, Orin and Rosa Kidd, are assigned to live and work at Korupun after Indonesian language study." Wonderful! The teammates I needed! Though I would have to slow down what little Scripture translation I was doing so I could write language lessons for them, giving the Kidds a faster start that way would be a joy—a happy part of the few months remaining before my home-country break (furlough) of several months. My first four years in Irian Jaya were about to close, and my first furlough break would start with fun.

Mission leaders suggested a travel route back to the US that would give me help as I traveled. It involved connecting with people in London and then on to New York. Mom told some of her close friends my route, and they insisted she should join me in London for a couple weeks' tour in the UK. They helped her get all her papers to do so. I could have run for joy up a cliff when I read her letter saying yes. Mom had not one adventurous bone in her body, but for my sake was willing to poke through her fears.

Anticipating that task-free happy time with Mom carried me along the final high-pressure months. Some of it, though, was the kind of soul-filling experience that I imagine only initial explorers get to have.

On one such day, I was just above the lowlands south of Korupun at about 1,000 feet elevation. Larry, the helicopter pilot, and I found a place by a riverbank to sit and wait while two Kimyals went into the jungle to try to contact the Giribun people and maybe even get some language data. As I sat there, I wrote a letter to Mom and described the sights, sounds, and my thoughts.

> I don't often get all worked up about all the strange things and doings out here, but besides us, probably the only other eyes in the world who have seen this same spot and the only other bodies who have sat on this log have been those of the local people. I will probably never again in my life be here. I'll probably never again see this same place, hear these gurgles of the river, or watch the butterflies flitter among these fern palms and trees. I'm content to sit and drink it all in. I have that "at-home feeling" that I always do in the lowlands.

Maybe the at-home feeling was the comfort of spending extended time alone with just my thoughts, away from the constant press of people needing my attention.

We never did contact any Giribun dwellers before the weather window to get back to Korupun closed. We left with no language data gathered. I would have to try to send messages to ask them to send one or two representatives on the four-day walk to Korupun so I could get data that way.

Back at Korupun, I packed for furlough and talked with the Kimyals who came to my door to sell something, ask me something, tell me something, or just chat.

Orin and Rosa Kidd would arrive in Sentani in a month; then they would come into Korupun for two months of orientation before going to Indonesian language school on another island. The McLeays would be back at Korupun to say goodbye and pack up their things during those two months, so the Kidds would live in my house. I needed to leave out some things for them to use. Good. Time saved. My mission agency's standard rule was that we had to pack away everything in fifty-five-gallon steel sealed drums and store them upstairs before a furlough of usually ten to twelve months.

With the Kidds coming, the McLeays leaving for good, and more tribal area being reached, things are changing—again. What will my next term hold? For sure not another year on my own.

Chapter 43

NEW TEAMMATES, NEW PROGRESS

By September 1978, I was back in Irian Jaya and back at Korupun for another four-year term.

My first term had been filled with learning and adjusting and the kind of work that helped the learning.

What about this term? I wondered. *I will enjoy adjusting to new teammates, Orin and Rosa, and be able to get into translation more, I hope. I'll never stop learning, that's for sure.*

While I was on furlough, Orin and Rosa Kidd completed Indonesian language study and spent two months at Korupun with the McLeays so Orin and Rosa could learn what was involved in ministry there before the McLeays left. Bruce and Judy flew to New Zealand two days before I landed back in Irian Jaya and were never able to return to Irian Jaya to work.

The Kidds left Korupun for business and shopping for a few weeks on the plane in which I arrived. Even so, my house welcomed me with my bed freshly made, flowers in a vase, fire lit, my kerosene fridge lit, and bread and biscuits made and waiting. Wow.

We've only met face-to-face twice, but they did all this!

I got to work right away writing more Kimyal language lessons for the Kidds. The lessons were short sentences—things the Kidds would need to say or ask, and explanations for all the person-tense verb endings needed in common situations when they would carry on conversations. The Kimyals did not know Indonesian, so the Kidds needed to communicate in Kimyal as soon as possible. The Kimyals continually asked for the kind of Bible teaching and practical help that Orin and Rosa couldn't give yet because they didn't know Kimyal.

My new four-year term began as the last had ended. As before, each day contained something new—new adventures, new vocabulary, new grammar insight, new cultural understanding, new or deepened friendships, plus wars, dark heavy spirit activity in villages, personal spiritual oppression, disappointments, sorrows, emotional dark valleys, illness, and bright breakthroughs that brought hope and joy. My journals and letters home contain vivid stories of so many events I can't remember them all. I know them only through reading.

I began teamwork with the Kidds by interpreting for Orin when the Kimyal elders sometimes asked him to preach in church and for him in his discussions with the Kimyals or as he taught the elders and other potential church leaders each week. With the apostle Paul and his student-helper Timothy in mind, Orin chose the name Timothy Class for his class with elders and others. Orin's goal was to develop them into strong spiritual leaders, as Paul had done for Timothy. My role was to translate and type each passage—with Orin's questions—that Orin wanted to teach from. That stretched my Kimyal and expanded Orin's understanding, too, as he saw the Kimyal version of what he wanted to convey.

It was a great day, after some months, when Orin said, "I'm going to try to teach without your help now. Just translate and type the verses and questions." I still interpreted for other gatherings though.

As Orin got to know what the just-learning Kimyal church needed, he wanted to teach through whole books. He chose Titus first.

"*Yes!*" Whole books had been my translation aim all along. As I worked, my mind sometimes nearly despaired trying to find the right words, but my heart sang. I knew that as the translations were thoroughly taught, lives would change.

Another teammate joined us around the middle of my second term. Jessie Williamson moved from Karubaga to Korupun. She had followed all the news about Korupun and the Kimyals and offered to help us. "You have a huge area and population with far-flung areas without any medical service. I'm not good at language, but I feel I should come and do my best to learn enough to give medical help and to train Kimyal medical workers."

That was not a simple transition for Jessie. She had spent at least a dozen years in Irian Jaya at Karubaga among the Danis. The two tribes were different from each other in more ways than language. It would mean a lot of adjustment for her. Bravely, Jessie came and began to learn Kimyal in a sink-or-swim manner, taking over the clinic duties. Jessie lived with me at first, but it didn't take long to build her a house across the airstrip.

Chapter 44
MOM'S VISIT

As the Kimyal church grew, all in Kimyal-land was sunshine and glory, right? No, but as my second four-year term was about over, I saw evidence of more and more people being changed by Jesus, the Light. Ogwen and Neno stood out to me because I knew them.

Ogwen started doing housework for me when she was about fourteen, after she married Neno, a boy of sixteen. Neno had previously done my laundry and yard work. Village leaders ended Ogwen and Neno's employment after a few years when they stole some things. I saw them begin to live genuinely changed lives, following "Jesus's path."

At age fifteen, Ogwen had a baby boy, but something was wrong. Ogwen took her baby to Jessie. The little boy had no skull from above his ears and brow ridge; only skin covered his brain. Kimyal babies are kept and carried in net bags lined with leaves, grass, and pandanus-leaf rain capes for windbreak and rigidity so the bag doesn't squeeze the baby too much. But that was scant protection for this baby. Jessie didn't expect him to live for more than ten days.

Ogwen was heartbroken. Her love for her baby boy cut directly across Kimyal cultural values. Defective, unwanted, or the second-born of twin babies were always thrown into a cold, swift river. People taunted Ogwen, "Throw the baby into the river. He's no good." They told Ogwen and Neno, "It's your fault. It's punishment for stealing. Throw him away."

They ostracized Ogwen, the ultimate and worst sign of contempt endured in Kimyal culture. Neno quietly loved and supported his young wife. Day after day, I saw her on the trail without a companion. She worked her gardens with no one working beside her. Always her net bag was on her back, carrying her child. His unprotected brain often caused seizures, and Ogwen would rush him to Jessie. Jessie could do little for the baby, but she did try to calm and console Ogwen. Incredibly, the baby lived six weeks.

How did these teenagers carry such a huge burden, withstanding that tremendous cultural pressure? In the days of darkness before the gospel, it wouldn't have happened.

My mom got to see Ogwen and Neno's story play out. In 1982, this unadventurous person, at age seventy, gathered the courage to join me for the last six weeks of my second term. My mission agency handled her travel arrangements to travel with a group of college student interns.

I suspect Mom needed to see for herself that I was OK out there in the "wilds." Was I telling the truth when I said I was fine? I laughed as I watched her throw her adventure-avoiding caution off like an old coat. She rode side-saddle on a motorbike, took a dugout canoe ride across a river, traveled by tiny helicopter through the mountains, walked along steep mud-slick trails with the Kimyals holding her hands to help, and got involved in not only my daily life but the Kimyals' as well.

After Mom's six weeks, we left together for my home leave. I knew that now when Mom read my letters or heard my stories, she would better understand what was in them.

Chapter 45

SIUD, A CHANGEMAKER

I had once wondered how God would lift the deep satanic darkness the Kimyals lived under. The kind of darkness that caused the irate man to kill the little boy, and the young man to sit on a fire unable to get off, and made mothers throw some babies in a river and caused clan wars and all manner of despair. The light came through men Orin mentored: Siud, Semia, and others.

Siud was the elder I felt the closest to. His wife, Yaso, became my regular house helper. Siud helped some, too, in the beginning. He was wonderfully comfortable in my house. Hungry to learn God's Word, Siud often walked in, sat in the chair by the little wood-burning heating stove in my tiny sitting room, and studied the Timothy Class materials. As Yaso became my friend as well as a helper, Siud also became a friend. His spiritual growth mirrored and often led the tribe's walk with the Lord.

I heard the beginning of Siud's story near the end of my time in Papua when one day Siud came into my office to visit and told it to me. This is how I remember it:

"My father was a shaman, big in this valley. I am Oldest Son, so when I was still a boy, my father began to train me to be a shaman too. He showed me what a shaman had to do to appease the ancestor spirits and other spirits so they wouldn't kill us. But my heart was troubled. 'Why must we always fear this anger and appease? Is there not freedom from the fear?'

"I often sat alone on a ridge where I could see mountain ranges, the sun, garden areas on the mountainsides, trees in the forests, rivers and waterfalls, and at night I saw the moon and stars. All those things sustained our lives.

"One day I understood in my heart that there must be a God who loves us. One day I would find out about him.

"I went to my father and told him, 'No. I will not become a shaman. Do not teach me anymore. I will wait to learn about the God who loves us and made all these things for us.'"

The rest of Siud's story I learned in pieces from various people during my time at Korupun.

In 1963 when Bruno deLeeuw and Phil Masters came over the rim of the Korupun Valley and realized that they had found the eastern tribe they were looking for, Siud was prepared for the truth they brought.

Warriors bristling with bows, arrows, and intimidating body decoration met Bruno and Phil. The warriors speculated, "Are these not ancestor spirits come into our realm? They have pale skin and are covered in spiders' webs (the closest thing they knew that looked like Western clothes). They must be."

At night in the men's huts, Kimyal men debated what they should do about Phil and Bruno. They couldn't trust the pale men, that was for sure. When Phil and Bruno offered the men salt, only one, a boy, was brave enough to try it. Siud. Everyone expected he would die.

"He did not die, but that does not tell us who they are," the men agreed.

As Phil and Bruno began to buy land to build a rough shelter and carve out an airstrip, more discussion in men's huts led to the conclusion: "They come from the spirits. We must offer them to the spirits as we do 'possums and other spirit totems. Tie them up and hang them in the rafters of a spirit hut until they die and their fat drips into the fire. That will appease the spirits."

"Why didn't they do that?" I asked the woman who told me this piece of the story. She shrugged her shoulders. "Why didn't they?"

Later, I heard that a small boy, Senenob, begged the men to let Phil and Bruno live. "I want to learn what they will teach." The Kimyal men listened to the boy.

Bruno went back to his family at Ninia, and Phil finished the airstrip. When the strip was approved for landing, Phil's wife, Phyliss, and their four children joined him at Korupun. Unknown to them, the Kimyals had planned to kill Phil and all his family when the family got out of the airplane. But Phyliss stepped out wearing a red dress. "Red! The good color. It's an omen. If we kill them, the spirits will do us bad. Tell everyone not to shoot," the war leader ordered. Phil and Phyliss knew none of this.

Later, Phil also flew in a few Dani missionaries. The ones who lived near Siud's village saw that Siud was a sickly, malnourished child, and often invited him to eat potatoes with them. He was with them anyway, as much as he could be, helping them learn Kimyal and hearing from them the words about Sky Father, "Eim Ayong," the God who loved them. As Siud's body grew stronger, he also grew strong in seeing that the words about God were true.

In September 1968, Yali men in the Yali's Seng Valley killed Phil and friend Stan Dale. Phyliss and her children went back to Karubaga where they had worked before, and Paul and Kathryn Kline came from Karubaga to Korupun to keep the work going until permanent missionaries could come.

Like Phil, Paul knew the Dani language and so was able to counsel and guide the Dani missionaries. He also learned to communicate in Kimyal.

When I joined the Klines at Korupun, Siud was a married young man with two small children. I did not know about him until I heard Paul express his worry after Siud's eighteen-month-old daughter died of pneumonia. Paul said, "Siud's heart is broken. He has gone to his far garden hut away from everyone and everything. He is mad at everything, including God. I hope he doesn't turn his back on God."

Siud was gone for two weeks, and when he came back, he was strong again in his love for God. His faith crisis strengthened him: he was more committed than ever to follow God's path.

By the time Orin and Rosa came, Siud was hungry to learn all he could about God. My memory can't say for sure, but I would not be surprised if it was Siud who, before the Kidds arrived, begged me to translate God's Word for them, saying, "We hunger for God's Word as we hunger for gwaneng [sweet potatoes]." It sounds exactly like Siud.

One day, Siud said to Orin, "I understand now! Each of us should teach another these things God says. First, I must teach my wife. Yaso must know God's words too."

Kimyals never let women know the "inner words" of their religion. They had an exclusively male side-language that kept women from understanding what they might overhear men discussing. Women, the men thought, could not be trusted with deep knowledge. They might use it against the men, causing cosmic environmental disasters that would endanger the tribe's survival.

Soon another man, Senenob, the now grown-up boy who had begged that Phil and Stan be spared, also began to teach his wife and even helped her to become a follower of Jesus.

Siud and Senenob taught their wives what Orin had explained to the men; they used Scripture and its application, including that people who are not yet following Jesus can't be expected to behave like they are.

This was a giant step in a culture that had strictly followed the rules of the spirits, under the threat of death for transgression. During Phil's time at Korupun, some who became Christians died at the hands of the spirit-worshipers so that the spirits would not bring revenge for the Christians' rebellion upon everyone else. Now this darkness was losing its grip.

But does evil easily surrender to the good and true? Does it fight on? As we worked, I often felt darkness push back, even as I saw light shining into the blackness.

Each week I translated for Orin in meetings with elders, in Timothy classes and random meetings with individuals, and for Orin's occasional sermons in church. At home, I translated the passages and questions for the Timothy classes and slowly made my way through Titus. Exhaustion crept in on me.

Besides Scripture translation, earth tremors, clan wars, language learning, a draining load of daily responsibilities, and the unexpected were still part of everyday life. Not one day went exactly as I planned. Multiply what I experienced during my first term, and you'll get the picture.

As the Kidds, Jessie, and I got to know each other, we also had fun times together—meals, games, visits, prayer, hikes among the villages and around the mountainsides, our own "church." There were always things to laugh about. Things like:

A new pilot, Larry, had been checked out at Korupun, but he was not allowed to land with full loads until he got a good feel for the approach and airstrip. The first time Larry landed after that restriction was lifted, he asked me, "How did my landing look?"

"Well, the Kimyals asked, 'Is he an ignorant one?'"

Larry made a big deal about that, and when he took off, Orin got on the ground-to-air radio and said, for all missionaries on the island to hear, "The Kimyals said that was the most ignorant takeoff they've ever seen."

"You turkey! They did not!" Larry answered.

Orin was an effectively methodical, patient teacher. In the beginning, as he went over questions during a Timothy Class, the men would sit mutely until someone said, "We don't know the answer. We're like children. You must tell us." To that, Orin always replied, "No. The answer is in the verses. Read them. Think. Find the answer and tell me." He waited until someone did. In this way, they gained confidence that they could, after all, understand God's Word themselves.

Slowly, elders and new pastors began to understand, teach, and preach with new confidence, and church attendance grew from the

Korupun Valley to all connected valleys south to the lowlands—half of the Kimyal tribe. More individuals came to understand the gospel and began to follow the Jesus Trail.

The thrill of watching that change still lights up my heart.

Chapter 46

NURSE ELINOR

I was relieved when, before Jessie came, Rosa took over the medical part of the daily routine, and it relaxed us both when Jessie moved to Korupun.

When Jessie came, we built a little clinic building to handle the steady stream of people needing medical attention. When neither Jessie nor Rosa was on station, though, for an hour each morning the locals had to endure the fact that I was out of practice. Yes, endure. One morning I especially felt like a klutz at the clinic.

A young boy was on a course of penicillin, and I had to give him his shot. I drew up a syringe of oily penicillin, stuck the needle in, pushed the plunger, and the needle separated from the syringe under the pressure, with a "flupf." I pulled out the needle and wiped off the blob of penicillin, which looked like a hunk of whipped cream sitting there on his bottom. I pulled up a new syringe, this time with regular procaine penicillin, and tried again. This time it separated with a "pop" and the contents, being watery, splattered all over. It hit my face, temporarily blinding me. I'm sure I absorbed some through my eyeballs, but the third time all went well. Poor kid. His mom told him it was all his fault for whimpering, so that third time he didn't let out a peep.

Another time, a man waited for me to see him standing outside my kitchen window. He held up his right hand.

"Eleenod," he pleaded, "Help me. I made a sore on my hand."

Yes, he "made a sore!" He cut it deep and clean across the palm with a machete. I didn't see that at first because of all the coagulated blood. I brought him inside and had him wash his hand under a faucet.

I cleaned it up, put the antiseptic, Bactine, on it, then applied a sterile dressing and wrapped a tight bandage around it all. The wound should have been stitched, but I was out of practice, it was in an awkward place, and the skin there looked very tough. The cut was the deepest right on the heel of the palm.

All the while, he was as calm as if I were dressing a scratch. I was calm knowing Jessie would return in the morning.

Sometimes my amateur nursing was successful, as when I stitched a boy's all-but-severed earlobe back in place, and it healed fine. And when I successfully helped a woman during a miscarriage. Blood and gore didn't bother me, and on one level I enjoyed my "doctoring," but I doubt that the Kimyals did.

Chapter 47
A PEOPLE TRANSFORMED

More than once people have asked me, "How did you make the Kimyals change?" My answer is, "You mean change from living in fear of the evil darkness they lived in to following Christ? Are you kidding? How could we convince anyone that hundreds of years of their ancestors' teaching are wrong—we, who are outsiders? Besides, not being cultural insiders, we did not know what was Kimyal culture unconnected to animistic beliefs and what was true worship of evil spirits. Only the Holy Spirit working in Kimyal hearts could do that."

The people of the Sela system of valleys and villages did not accept hearing about the gospel as readily as the Korupun area people did. When Orin began his Timothy classes at Korupun, there were Dani missionaries in the northern part of Sela, but in the south and eastern Sela, the people were serious in their death threats toward any evangelist who dared enter their territory. Even in the northern area, defiance was palpable.

The trail over the mountain between Korupun and Sela Valleys peaked at about 10,000 feet and took eight to ten hours to cross.

Late one Saturday afternoon, a messenger arrived from Sela with news that the eastern Sela village of Eyub had surrounded, ambushed, ransacked, and burned Orisin, a village in northern Sela.

Early in the morning, the Eyub men had ringed Orisin "and waited for the people to go out with their pigs or to do feces or urine," a Kimyal reported. Eyub men seriously wounded three people. The man wounded the worst was newly baptized. For a long time, Eyub and two other villages opposed to the gospel had threatened, "We're going to kill the baptized people." But this was more complicated than a case of non-Christians attacking Christians.

Many years earlier, even before the gospel came, men from Orisin ambushed and killed a big chief from the eastern Sela villages of Eyub and Meigum. Years later those villages were still fighting in a never-ending revenge struggle. In one attempt to stop the fighting, Dani evangelists broke the bows of the Eyub men and took a few pigs. Pigs are the highest valued possession of a Kimyal. Though someone paid for the pigs later, that was not enough to quench the smoldering resentment. At that time, it was still a high Kimyal virtue to hold a grudge and get revenge.

Not long before this incident, some men from Eyub stole an Orisin woman as part of the payback for wrongs done to them. When some Orisin men and Dani evangelists went to Eyub to discuss this, the Eyub men said, "We'll cut you open and see what is really in your hearts."

One of the Danis stretched out his hands and said, "Go ahead. Tie me up." But one of the Eyub men replied, "Just go home. We'll fight."

And so the attack that Saturday morning.

A core element in all of this is that these hostile people gave the label "Christian" to anyone who was baptized, wore clothes, or came "from the sky" (in an airplane or helicopter). In their minds, all Korupun people were Christians. Not only was that far from true but also only a few who were Christian wore clothes. Few Orisin people were Christians at that time.

Soon after the ambush of Orisin, some of its men captured an Eyub man, stretched his arms and legs out like they would a pig, and shot three arrows into him.

Other villages in the Sela Valley half of the tribe were also fighting each other. It seemed the whole place was in an uproar.

We knew that darkness was fighting hard to keep the Light away. However, the fighting created a flood of refugees who came over that difficult trail to Korupun and therefore to the Light of God. The very people whom the darkness hated, the Jesus followers of Korupun, welcomed, fed, and housed all the refugees—at least two or three hundred people. These Korupun Christians even went up the trail to meet families and helped carry children, burdens, and the elderly.

So it was that, despite setbacks and failures, even among its leaders sometimes, the Kimyal church continued to grow. It grew in numbers as more and more people stepped onto the path of following Jesus, but it also grew in learning what a walk with Jesus means and in shaping their lives that way. One by one, the few became many, and leaders began to mature. Siud was one of those leaders.

From Orin's earliest days at Korupun, he saw God's invisible hand on Siud. When he could, Orin took Siud with him to villages to help teach.

During a time when it was safe to walk over the trail to Sela and back, Orin invited Siud and other emerging leaders to go with him to teach and encourage the evangelists in Sela. Along the trail, they met and chatted with two withered old women. Characteristically, the women flattered Orin, their "father," telling him, among other compliments, how good he was.

After leaving the women, Orin asked Siud, "What did Jesus tell us to do in Matthew 28?"

"Go and tell all people about him."

"Right. Does that mean just speaking to crowds? We could have spoken about him to those two women back there."

"Yes! I could have told them that they shouldn't call you good. Only God is good."

The next time they met people on the trail, while Orin was talking with a couple, he heard another two tell Siud how good Orin was. Siud at once replied, "My friend, don't call Orin good. Only God is good," and he went on to teach them about Jesus.

When they reached Sela, Orin and Siud stayed a few days in a cabin there, and one evening a man came to visit. Orin needed

Siud's help to supply words when he was stuck as he explained the gospel story to their visitor. The next day, at an impromptu outdoor meeting, Siud preached and went right down the line of what he had helped Orin explain the night before.

During that visit to Sela, as Light penetrated, darkness pushed back. Once, warriors, all decked out and fully armed, barred the trail, so Orin and the others had to take a different path than planned.

Across the valley from where the Korupun men stayed, one village stated their resistance to the gospel another way: they killed and ate a woman. They knew that Orin and the other men could see the smoke and hear the dancing. The invisible struggle between darkness and Light became visible that day.

Chapter 48

A GROWING CHURCH

Over the years as individuals grew in their knowledge of God, the collective groups of believers grew.

A pivotal point was one weekend when all churches in the Korupun Valley and some farther out flooded in for the installation of the first official Kimyal pastor and assistant: Semia as pastor and Siud as his assistant.

On Saturday, men brought squealing pigs that were hung upside down from poles and tied on with ropes around their feet. Other men stacked rocks on giant piles of wood. As they lit the wood on fire, the rocks popped and exploded with heat. Every explosion induced whooping and whistling from the men preparing the pits. More pig squeals echoed through the valley as arrows hit the pigs. Their blood was caught to make blood-and-fat sausage. Men singed the pigs' hair off, then butchered and laid the parts in the pits. They added chickens, sweet potatoes, candle vegetables, taro, sweet potato leaves, other greens, maize, chayote, and other vegetables in the pits, then covered them in banana leaves and dirt. Finished with making the slow cookers in the ground, the people left the food to steam while they gathered for a service on the airstrip.

Rain began as the service ended, but that could not dampen the excitement as people opened the pits and distributed the food.

The next day, Sunday morning, enthusiasm remained high as people scoured the valley, including the missionaries' yards, for flowers and foliage to decorate the church. Red is every Kimyal's favorite color. Poinsettias were one flower missionaries could plant with success. We had many poinsettia bushes at Korupun, and they appeared abundantly in the decorations.

When everything was ready, people began to gather, and soon the church was full. Everyone sat on the floor as always, packed skin-to-skin. After Kimyal-style chanting of some hymns and a few Indonesian-style songs, Orin challenged the two men to take their duties seriously. He similarly challenged their wives and the congregation.

Siud, the assistant pastor, gave his response first, then Semia, the pastor. They accepted the positions with soft voices and solemn faces. They said they couldn't do the job without God and asked the people to pray for them. When the two men finished, Orin and the elders put their hands on the heads of Siud and Semia and asked God to guide them as they guided the village churches.

Then everyone left the building and went to the airstrip where they could spread out for a communion service. This installation of the first two Kimyal pastors was a milestone of the Lord's building of his church among the Kimyals.

Siud was just one among other elders and pastors who, like dry moss in a downpour, soaked up what they heard and read of God's Word and applied it the Kimyal way.

Nevertheless, even God's people like Siud may make bad choices.

Siud and his younger brother, Bogso, didn't get along very well. I didn't hear about their spats from them, but rather from others. They lived in the same small village, and in that face-to-face culture, everyone knew everyone else's business.

One day I heard that Siud and Bogso had been in a mud-slinging fight. Kimyals grab handfuls of mud to hurl at each other until both are coated with it. While at it, they also hurl insults. It wasn't a fight with sticks, rocks, or machetes, but in Kimyal culture, it was major.

The church leaders took the incident seriously. Siud had disgraced the reputation of the Lord. Though he was ashamed, the tribe needed to see that this kind of behavior was not acceptable for anyone claiming to follow Jesus, and certainly not for a pastor. So they decided that Siud would not preach for nine months.

I thought this was a little severe, but Siud quietly accepted the restriction as a just consequence. Looking back, I think the whole incident made the validity of his leadership stronger by example.

In fact, in a way, Siud's failure and restoration mirrored that of the whole Kimyal church through the years since then and even now. They saw that failure need not be permanent: deal with the consequences and move on, stronger.

Chapter 49

BATTLES WITH DISEASE AND DEPRESSION

As more and more Kimyals began to follow God, or "take God's Word" as they would say; as church leaders grew; as I worked on never-ending language analysis and Bible translation; as I trained Kimyal adults how to teach children Bible stories and truths—other duties piled up. I hosted missionaries, other visitors, and Bible college summer interns and planned the learning and practical help experiences of the interns. I still worked on things like station bookkeeping, what goes into living without Western conveniences, and discussions with the Kimyals about a variety of problems.

Sometimes I left Korupun to take in a linguistic/translation workshop, or teach VBS for another mission's conference, or go to Sentani to use the computers in SIL's new computer lab to type the translations I had done so they could be printed.

It was on one of those trips to the coast during my second four-year term that our field chairman, Graham Cousens, asked me to come to his office to chat and catch up.

His eyes showed care and concern. "You are overtired, and for good reason. You are doing too much, too hard. You need a break, or you're going to crash."

"But how is it all going to get done if I don't keep at it? The Kimyals need more Scripture—yesterday. And we need a correct analysis of Kimyal phonetics to teach new readers an orthography (alphabet system) that fits. They are begging for new reading primers that we're not ready to give. I can't take a break now."

I had two Kimyal language helpers with me. Three days a week we would all take a half-hour morning taxi ride to where I rented time at the SIL computer and language lab. It was stifling hot there on the coast, and the lab wasn't air-conditioned. We mountain dwellers weren't used to that, but we pushed through until about 3:00, then would take a taxi back to our hotel/guest facility. I gave the guys the rest of the day off, but I kept working until 6:00 each of those days, as well as on the days in between our trips to the lab, except for Sundays.

One Sunday evening at the English language church, I couldn't sing during the hymns. I felt like I was going to burst into tears any second. I choked down sobs, fortunately not noticed during the singing. The next day I forced myself to work some more, but on Tuesday I couldn't. Slight pain low under my right ribs in the morning grew to intense pain by evening. Dr. Liz Cousens, who was also in Sentani for business, felt that area and said I had a swollen liver. She didn't know the cause, but other tests showed it was probably Dengue fever. It doesn't often attack the liver, but in my case, in the weeks before, I had had both malaria and hepatitis, so my liver was weakened.

"Strict bed rest for several weeks until your liver goes down. This swelling is dangerous."

Graham Cousens arranged special semi-emergency flights to take me back to Korupun. He had been right. I had crashed.

First, Jessie was assigned to care for me at Korupun. Then I was to go to Sue at Soba, then back to Korupun, to Jessie's house. I stayed with them so they could watch the size of my liver and make sure I was down more than I was up and did nothing strenuous. At first, they allowed me up only for the bathroom or a quick shower. A huge book, the biography of Charles Spurgeon, was my diversion. It especially helped on the every-other-days of depression that are typical of Dengue fever.

During those several weeks of imposed rest, I learned what I would need to know ten years later: God is not tied to our plans.

Was I indispensable to his plans for the Kimyals? Nope. It was *his* business, and he could change "my" place in his business whenever he wanted. And it would be for the eternally best outcome that only he knew.

After the "sentence" of imposed rest, Dr. Liz let me go back to my own house if I promised to take two-hour naps each afternoon for six weeks. Then, if my liver was average size, I could resume a regular schedule. My liver cooperated, and I gratefully got back to typical days.

My entire second term, I battled illnesses. Liver pain lingered in the background almost every day, and I went to bed exhausted every night. Twice malaria (despite prophylaxis) hit so hard that I could not walk more than a few feet, I was so weak.

One of those times occurred before Orin and Rosa left for their first leave to the US. That bout of malaria put me down in bed. The Kidds, the pastors, and the elders were so concerned for me that they asked if they could come and pray for me. Of course they could! That the Kimyals wanted to perform a pastoral role for me was beautiful.

I recovered and did not ever get such a bad case of malaria again. By my fourth term, I had no malaria at all and decided to experiment not taking preventive medication. Even without prophylaxis, I became free from attacks of malaria. I was one of a minority who builds an immunity to it. Because of the Kimyals' prayers?

Church leaders grew in confidence, and I continued translating, training, and more. As disorderly as it seemed, it all brought me joy.

Until a cloud lowered.

———— ∞∞∞ ————

I don't know if it was depression or oppression, but I will never forget the blackness I fell under after the death of Momas, the shaman chief in the closest village, Maningmog. Momas had faraway gardens across the deep south gorge and up the facing mountain. When anyone went to their far gardens, they stayed there in a rough shelter for two or three days. Four days went by since Momas left for his far gardens, and villagers were concerned. Two men set out to check on him. Late in the day, they came back, carrying his body on a makeshift litter. They had found Momas dead on the mountainside. The village loudly wailed late into the night and began wailing again in the morning. Momas had been a strong leader, a powerful shaman, and a feared man.

I was starting my day when Orin came. "Pray for me," he said. "Men from Maningmog came and said that Momas's body is doing strange things. They want me to come and see."

When Orin returned, he told me what was going on. It looked like evil spirits were leaving Momas's convulsing dead-cold body, and they were not happy about leaving.

The next few weeks after the cremation of Momas, people reported seeing spirits in their gardens, hearing scratching on the outside of their huts at night, and feeling a sense of heaviness.

I felt it too. I fell into a deep depression. Thoughts came that told me, "You are a failure. Everyone knows your translations are iffy, your language analysis is poor, and the Kimyals don't like you. Your missionary colleagues don't respect you either. You can't do this job. Just give up."

My Bible training kicked in. I knew that if Satan is "the father of lies," the members of his gang are liars too. The ones newly without a human host in the valley would love to see me, a member of Jesus's team, give up. "God," I prayed, "win this battle, lift the darkness, and bring back the light." In a few weeks, the heaviness left.

That was my most profound time of depression, and it taught me that God is with us in those times too. My earlier experience with the every-other-day emotional slumps of Dengue fever helped me. I knew to stay calm, ride it out, and know that it would not last.

Chapter 50

TRANSLATING BIBLE BOOKS AND STORIES

After Orin and Rosa joined me at Korupun, at first what I translated was what Orin felt the emerging church leaders needed. Some days, even while I ate my supper, I worked on part of a New Testament chapter that Orin wanted me to translate for his next few discipleship class sessions. For example, when Orin started to teach about elders—what they are to be and to do—he chose parts of 1 Timothy 3, Titus 1, and Ephesians 4, which teach concepts like being temperate.

I wasn't far enough along in Kimyal myself to know how to say "temperate," let alone other behavior concepts. But I kept working on it until I got what Orin could at least test and see if the guys understood correctly. What a mind stretcher. I had a copy of Titus that had been translated from Dani by one of our local fellows, but it was a third-order (from Greek to English to Dani to Kimyal) translation and therefore far from the original. With two Indonesian translations and five English translations spread out in front of me, plus good English and Greek reference books, I changed most of it. I tried to grasp the concept of the original and then put it into the framework of Kimyal words and thoughts.

That is when I realized I needed to start learning Greek, which I hadn't been able to do during my college years. I heard about a seminary that offered Greek by correspondence and added that to my pile of "things to do."

I never knew what a day might hold, but my plan was always to get as much translation done as I could. Sometimes that was

RUNNING ON BROKEN LEGS

pencil drafts on my own, sometimes I reworked those with a Kimyal helper, sometimes I read a draft with a group who had not heard or seen any of it so I could discover problem areas. I made the noted changes and typed that section or chapter to give to pastors and elders to teach and preach from. Then, if they preached from a test copy of a Scripture book, I listened to what they taught to see if they understood the passage correctly.

My hand-typed Gestetner mimeograph stencils of the pages of the books of Titus, 1 John, and other small books looked like they had measles, there were so many pink typo correction spots on them. Then came the jobs of cranking pages out, cutting the resulting paper sheets in half, assembling them, adding heavier stock paper covers, and stapling them into books. I couldn't just fly to the coast to use the SIL (Wycliffe) computer lab each time I wanted to test out a few small books.

A plan took shape in my head. I decided that during my second furlough, I would take a few computer classes at Whitworth College and somehow come up with the money to buy and ship the type of computer and printer SIL used. One that could take the tropical humidity.

I began that furlough break with a live report to my church. As I talked about the growth of the Kimyal church and my progress in Bible translation, I showed slides of the area and people. Among those who heard and saw my report was former Riverside Highschool classmate, Mike Johnson, and his family. Mike was a self-employed site-specific mini-hydro maker and installer. When he saw my slides, he was amazed by all the waterfalls on the cliffs surrounding Korupun Valley. "Perfect for a mini-hydro," he thought. "The question isn't if there is a spot for it, but which spot would be the best."

Later, Mike asked me, "Would a mini-hydro at Korupun help you?" Would it ever! We had a diesel-powered generator that we ran when it was dark from 6:00–9:00 only. Fuel was expensive to buy and to fly in. Would free electricity be helpful? Yes! So we began to make long-range plans.

Just buying and shipping the computer and printer in those days cost about $20,000.

How was I going to find that much money?

I did not want to ask my supporting churches and people to give more than they were.

I prayed, "Lord, this is your project. I will not mention it to my supporters. If you want me to have the computer equipment, prompt the pastors or individuals to ask if I have any extra needs. Then I'll tell them about the hydro project."

As far as I remember, every church asked that question. By the end of my ten-month furlough, I had all the money I needed. I ordered the equipment and arranged to ship it to Irian Jaya.

All the money came from tiny churches and regular people. God did it! Mike took on the responsibility to raise money for the hydro project.

Chapter 51

A HYDRO PLANT FOR KORUPUN

In June 1983, I returned to Korupun, this time accompanied by Mike Johnson and twelve-year-old David. The plan was for Mike to choose the best waterfall-created stream where there was a good place for a holding pond and a downhill grade where pipes could carry fast-running water to a generator.

That done, Mike and David returned to Chattaroy, and Mike began to draw up plans for the generator and for the logistics of getting it, pipe, and other equipment shipped to Irian Jaya then flown to Korupun.

In the meantime, I resumed Bible translation and produced preliminary editions of Bible books as I had done before by manual typewriter and a hand-cranked mimeograph machine. By October 1983, I had put the book of Ephesians through several revisions and was waiting for our field's translating committee approval to print and distribute it. In November, they approved the printing of 200 copies of Ephesians. I typed the Gestetner stencils for the book, and some guests of Orin and Rosa turned the Gestetner handle countless times to run them off and then assembled them.

That finished, I concentrated on translating the book of Luke that I had started earlier. I knew it would take at least a year to finish, revise, and be ready for the preliminary printing of 200.

I hope I have my computer before many more months. It will make the process so much faster. With that equipment, I could correct text on-screen and print a few copies right away. If I needed several copies, the dot matrix printer could cut Gestetner stencils error-free and faster than hand-typing.

I don't have a record of the exact date, but sometime in March or April 1984, the computer and dot matrix printer cleared customs on the coast and waited for a flight to Korupun. In May, they came to Korupun. *Yeah!*

In October 1984, I got word: "The hydro pipes have cleared customs." The pipe sections were too long for the size of the airplanes that could land at Korupun, so the pipes were staged at Ninia, which had a longer airstrip, one a Cessna Commander could use. It was only a twenty-minute flight from Korupun. On American Thanksgiving Day 1984, a helicopter shuttled the pipes to Korupun.

Missionaries Art and Carol Clark worked in a small Yali Valley called Lolat. One shuttle trip swung by Lolat, picked up Art and Carol, and brought them to Korupun. Together we had a big, special Thanksgiving celebration.

We discovered that though the pipes were too long for a Cessna flight, they were shorter than ordered. For enough pipes to reach between the pond and the hydro unit, we needed more, so we had to wait for another shipment. In the meantime, Mike worked on making the hydro unit, and I ran our diesel generator to power my computer for only the time that I needed to type something into my computer or print something from it. I named my computer Sophie, after the Greek word *sophia*, which means wisdom.

My heart sped with joy as my printer ran off the final pages of the book of Luke. Later, the corrections suggested by my first Kimyal readers were easy to make. All twenty-four chapters were now ready to be printed for preliminary distribution. In early 1985, I sent the computer tape to our print shop in Sentani. What a joy! The print shop had the same kind of DEC computer that the SIL computer lab and I used. The floppy disks of other brands of computer wouldn't stand up to the heat and humidity of Irian Jaya, but the DEC tapes would. That was high tech in 1985.

A few years earlier, Paul and Kathryn Kline had moved to Sela Valley from Karubaga, wanting to be back helping the Kimyal people. The Korupun staff was not only happy for their help in the work but also for Paul's mechanical skill when we had problems with the generator. The Klines were eager to get copies of Luke for Sela too.

In April, the boxes of 200 copies of Luke came to Korupun from the print shop in Sentani. When the smaller box came to my house, I opened it. The Kimyals inside and outside my house burst with excitement. Nebyan, doing some outside work for me, said, "That's what I want for my pay!" Sa'ale bought one right away, and Yaso soon arrived saying, "I need some water for my jug—and the Luke books came? I want to buy one." I gave my garden worker, Asabing, a nine-pound box of the books to take over the trail to Paul Kline in Sela. That trail was so long, high, and difficult that we kept carriers' loads to under five kilos.

Two weeks after the boxes of Luke came, in May 1985, Paul came to overhaul and do general maintenance on the generator. Looking for motor parts, he opened the parts box of hydro-generator things and found a treasure. In that box were parts for an aluminum MTS carrier that could easily be taken apart and reassembled. It even had a model and serial number. Without telling me, he and some Kimyal helpers put it together, set a little boy in it, and carried him across the airstrip to my house. I knew something was up when I heard high excited chatter and saw a stream of men, women, and children coming.

That evening I wrote to Mom, "Call Mike and tell him 'Thank you *so* much for the MTS. I'll be going over to Sela in it one of these days, and it's what I've been waiting for.'"

Three months later, in August, Mike and Debi Johnson, their son David and their triplet daughters, Karen, Kelsie, and Krissy, arrived in Sentani. With them was a couple Mike had recruited to help, Hap and Linda Schnaze with their two children, Benny and Anna.

I met them all in Sentani. They got their temporary stay permits, and four days later we all flew to Wamena in a Commander and from there to Korupun in two smaller Cessnas. We landed in touch-and-go weather. I wrote to Mom, "I bet the pilots tried so hard because they didn't want their wives to have to feed and put up so many people for the night."

Mike and Hap started work at 7:00 the next morning. Whooping, hollering, loud chatter, and whistles filled the valley as Kimyal men carried the hydro turbine down to the previously prepared slab. What looked like a confusing mass of bosses all giving orders to each other soon got the turbine properly positioned. Mike and Hap hired boys to bring sand and gravel from the big river for making cement. Before long the turbine was cemented in place on the slab.

Over the next weeks, crews of Kimyals dug the ditch for the pipe, then helped to lay the pipe, glue sections together, set up poles, build the hydro shed, string wires, and all the other needed tasks. They ran electricity to the church building, the Bible school building, the clinic, and the missionaries' houses. Finally, the ribbon-cutting day came. Kimyals love ceremony. Despite the rain, a large crowd gathered at the hydro shed for the celebration.

As the work progressed, the Johnson and Schnaze children helped as they could but mostly played and explored the valley with the Kimyal children, learning some Kimyal language along the way.

After three weeks, the Johnson family left, but the Schnazes stayed on.

Mike had brought a movie camera to Korupun so he could shoot some movie film that would help him explain the project to friends of the venture. Back in Chattaroy, Mike heard about a film-productions college student who needed to do a thirty-minute film project to graduate. Mike contacted the young man, and he turned Mike's movie shots into a professional-quality production. Viewers were fascinated by the terrain and the Kimyal people. When they saw it, they knew exactly what the hydro project at Korupun had been and how badly it was needed.

Hap, still at Korupun, was a contractor and had come planning extra time to build a new office for me. The office in my house was way too small for the extra tables and shelves I needed for the computer, printer, scanner (planned but not bought yet), and books.

I had drawn plans for an office attached to a four-foot covered breezeway I would enter through a new door in my current office wall. I had ordered all the wood and supplies. With electricity now, Hap could use a few small power tools. Upscale!

That office became my translation haven. It was also a place where people could come directly into the office and discuss things in confidence. In my house office, translation helpers and others had to walk through the house to reach my office. Yaso, my house helper, loved the new setup.

Chapter 52

TRANSLATION STORIES

In later years, when the Kidds were on furlough break or when they left during the time their boys were in high school in the US, my daily three or more hours of translation time with Dayun and the local Bible school students was reduced as extra duties became mine. Church leaders needed to discuss issues; Rosa's weekly women's class for church leaders' wives became mine to teach; there was airstrip maintenance to supervise; the station store to stock and open once a week until I taught a Kimyal how to do it. The station store was an outlet where people could spend the money they earned working for us or selling us vegetables or firewood. It also got them familiar with an essential part of the world outside their mountain home. That foreign world would eventually come to their tribal area. They needed to be equipped to avoid being taken advantage of. I was also putting more language lessons together for Jessie so that she could handle the medical work better.

Even though those extra jobs cut down my time for translating, my heart sang at the translation progress. My goal was quality. I took as much time as I needed to produce the best translation I could at whatever stage of Kimyal knowledge I had. My local helpers were patient as we worked. They sensed and explained what I didn't understand clearly. They said, "Oh, we are scared. If this isn't right Kimyal, people will say, 'Who told her that way? They did bad!'"

To help my helpers grasp the concepts of Scripture translation, I took the two most dedicated helpers I had besides Dayun with me to United Bible Society or Wycliffe Bible Translators translation workshops.

—∞—

During one stretch, Dayun and I worked on one of the apostle Paul's letters for several weeks. In this biblical letter, how to translate the English word "mercy" was a huge problem. Not satisfied with my stabs at translating it, I tried several ways to explain the concept to Dayun so that she could give me a useful Kimyal equivalent. I had no success. A long phrase for the word would be too cumbersome for a new reader (which most Kimyals were) to read and still remember the context. But even brilliant Dayun couldn't grasp what I tried to explain. The top Kimyal cultural value was revenge. Revenge that could be owed for generations. Mercy, forgiveness, and related ideas didn't even exist. I had to skip over that paragraph and hope we would eventually find the answer.

One morning when Dayun came to work, her eyes shone with excitement.

"Did you hear what happened this morning?"

"No. Tell me!"

"You know how that men from Sela have been saying, 'Men who wear gourds are our friends; men who wear shorts are our food.' Well, they decided to attack Korupun. The Sela men snuck over the trail during the night for a surprise attack at dawn. But our church leaders heard about the plan and decided what to do.

"Before dawn, our leaders went up past Segeddam. They chose a spot where they could hide in bushes on both sides of the trail, then waited with bows and arrows for the Sela men to come.

"When the Sela men were in the right spot, our Korupun men jumped out of the bushes with their bows drawn and surrounded the Sela men. The Sela men knew they would be shot and were so scared they shook, their gourds flew off, and they urinated all over.

"When the Sela men were greatly scared, our men said, 'In the name of Jesus, we relax the bow,' and they all did."

I interrupted, "Dayun! That's it! Those words are what I have tried to find. Relax the bow. That's what God did because Jesus took what we deserved. We deserved death, but God relaxed the bow drawn against us. We're free."

In Kimyal culture, before the gospel came, mercy had never been an option. This was an incident of powerful mercy. Light again pierced darkness.

When mercy is extended, peace can come. *Peace* was another word I had to fish for. I asked Semia questions and described hypothetical situations which would hopefully give me just the right term for the kind of *peace* I needed for the passage I was working on.

Have you ever noticed how many kinds of peace there are in the English language? Everything from inner calmness to reconciled enemies. There are many kinds of peace in Kimyal, too, and there is no single word for *peace*. Instead, they have very colorful, descriptive phrases for each specific incident. One phrase is "stomach flat in." As they see it, one's stomach sticks out when he is upset. Another is "each becoming at the same place." That is, two people coming to an agreement and thus becoming at peace with each other. Another is "eating the kidney of the arrow," the expression used when warring parties have made a peace pact. Can you imagine your country's leader talking about eating the kidney of their war arsenal?

———

So it was that bit by bit I made progress. On Sundays, I took a notebook and pencil with me to church so I could not only jot down new (to me) words and phrases but also note whether the translation caused any wrong ideas.

Early on I saw the need for the Kimyals to know the Old Testament stories that formed the basis for New Testament truth. Wycliffe Bible Translators had developed a good English language summary of the Old Testament—one made to use especially in tribal contexts. So I began to work through an Old Testament summary in Kimyal, as well as the New Testament translation. I noticed right away how the stories of Genesis and Exodus, about the tribes of Israel, bow-and-arrow fights, and simple dwellings, fit right into a Kimyal-like context.

The summaries of Leviticus and Numbers were a unique challenge. Even we English speakers, with all the help available to us, have problems understanding the sacrifices, feasts, and ceremonies. Putting it all into clear Kimyal, even in summary form, stretched my ability to be creative in the language, but that was fun.

Some days I focused on translating the Bible Visuals International illustrated stories that a few men, at first, taught children on Sundays in a sort of Sunday school held while adults were in church. After translating the stories, I taught them to the teachers. The kids loved them, eagerly learned the memory verse, and looked forward to next week's story.

Senenob and Senebing were the first men I taught to do that. Sometimes they needed a break and asked me to tell the story.

One such Sunday I used a flannelgraph story of the Good Samaritan—the story of the man from Samaria being robbed and beaten, then left to die beside the road. Saturday, as I was practicing the story with Senenob as my audience, he got all upset at the priests and Levites leaving the poor man to die. Senenob began laughing in embarrassment for them. Senenob had an infectious laugh and he got me going too. So there we were, the pair of us, sitting in front of the flannel board laughing while the poor man was stuck up there dying. As Senenob laughed, he bit his knuckles in Kimyal fashion and said, "Oh, pity! Pity!"

When I told the story to the kids on Sunday, there were comments throughout, but they got the biggest kick out of the Samaritan putting the guy on his donkey and going down the trail. There were no donkeys or other ridable animals in all of Papua, so the children found that hilarious. Times like this are why I sometimes gave in to the desire to teach the lesson.

Chapter 53
KIMYAL MISSIONARIES

As my Kimyal helpers and I wrote and distributed more Old Testament story summaries and New Testament books, Korupun men wanted to spread this good news to more of their people. At a time when the church in the upper Sela area was growing but wasn't yet mature enough to see the need to tell other areas about Jesus, and when Orin and Rosa were on home leave, a few Korupun elders came to me and said, "We want to go to villages in eastern Sela and see if they will accept a teacher of Jesus's words. In the past, we were enemies, so they may not be friendly and feed us. Will you give us salt, razor blades, and matches to buy potatoes? Also, rice and pots to cook in?" I gladly did.

The delegation was gone for about a week. When the group returned, they told me about the trip.

"The faces of the men were heavy toward us. Their spirits were hard. They would not give us food or listen to our words. The night before we were going to come back, a boy snuck into the house where we were and told us, 'Leave in the dark by another trail. The big men plan to ambush and kill you on the trail tomorrow. I heard them say this.' So as soon as the village was asleep, we crept out of our hut and came along the bad trail—the hard way no one takes. There are many rocks and steep places to climb, and much mud. It takes a long time, and we became exhausted. But Sky Father protected us, just as he did when he sent that little boy to warn us."

The issue for the murder plot wasn't merely the Korupun elders' talk about God. It was also that, contrary to the rules of the ancestor spirits, they had cooked their sweet potatoes in the pots I gave them, not in the ashes. Every Kimyal knew that the ancestor spirits had commanded them to cook sweet potatoes in the ashes of their fires. If anyone disobeyed, the spirits would cause a blight or drought to come on all gardens. In the resulting famine, everyone would starve to death. That Sela village was still under the darkness of fear of the ancestral spirits. To prove that they did not condone the Korupun men's way of cooking potatoes in this village, the Sela men had to kill them. Or try to.

Did the Korupun elders know this before they went? Of course. But they hoped for a break in the darkness. "We will pray, wait, and try again another time," they told me.

Remembering they were resistant to teaching about God in the beginning, too, the Kimyal elders were patient and didn't give up. Eventually, they were able to send missionaries to that area. Before that, though, they sent some south.

Some months after the failed attempt to contact the Giribun people who live in the lowlands next to the south side of the mountain range where the Kimyal tribe lives, a few Kimyal church leaders came to me with a request like their earlier appeal before the eastern Sela trip. "We want to walk down to Giribun and see if they will accept a Jesus teacher. Will you do the same as when we went to eastern Sela? Will you give us what we need to buy and cook food?"

That would be a four- or five-day walk, and the areas they walked through might not feed them well, so I gladly complied. We also prayed that this time, unlike before, they would have a successful contact with the Giribun people.

When the delegation returned, they reported to me, "We talked to them! They were friendly but don't want a teacher yet. We will pray for them. Another day they will want God's words." And they couldn't help adding, as they averted eye contact, but also half smiled, "they don't wear gourds."

"Oh, they don't? What do they wear then?"

Still semi-embarrassed but bursting to tell, they said, "They just wear leaves wrapped 'round."

Inwardly I grinned and thought, *Culture shock, guys. It's how some people react to your gourds!*

After Orin and Rosa returned from home leave, the European missionary to a lowland tribe west of Giribun heard that this tribe was thinking of receiving an evangelist. The missionary suggested to them that men from his area could come. However, Giribun balked at that because they were traditional enemies of the tribes west of them.

This issue started a discussion among the white missionaries, and they agreed that it was up to the Giribun people to decide who they wanted and when.

A year or two later, just before Christmas, a delegation of Giribun men trekked up to Korupun to ask Orin for Kimyal evangelists. This venture was their first-ever trip that far up into the highlands. I knew they were from Giribun when I saw one of them—sure enough, he just had a sort of leaf affair wrapped 'round. His tall, long-legged body, his facial features, and his skin disease also said that he was from the lowlands. What courage it must have taken for them to come almost 6,000 feet up into the cold highlands. The next day, the delegation members were all in shorts that Semia bought for them at our little trading store.

The Giribun men had a meeting with Orin. They named fourteen chiefs who wanted Kimyal men to go down and teach them God's words. We missionaries at Korupun agreed that we needed to back away and see if the Kimyal church would take the request to heart and send couples to Giribun. It was theirs to do and to decide when to do it.

Nine months later another delegation of twenty-five men from Giribun came up during an evangelists' conference. "We will not go back until you promise us some people to teach us about God," they said. So the Kimyal church chose Yaya and his wife from the Duram Valley as the evangelist and Nasa and his wife from the foothills of Deibula as their medical worker. The very first Kimyal missionaries.

Chapter 54

BAD LEGS

With their love of ceremony, the Kimyals had a big feast every time one of us missionaries came back to Korupun from furlough. So when I returned for my third term of four years, we enjoyed a valley-wide celebration: pit-cooked pork, chicken, sweet potatoes, other vegetables—the works. It was a warm, sunny day. I thoroughly enjoyed sitting by a pit oven visiting with the women and children around me.

Afterward, I noticed I was greeted with, "Hello, Bad Legs" or "Hello, Bad Legs Woman." Previously one or two had done that now and then, but now everyone said that all the time and looked so pleased when they used the name.

But what, I pondered, *is the real significance of my new name?*

That I had "bad" legs was clear, but I knew the name must have more significance than the obvious. In Western culture, Bad Legs might be a derisive name, but I knew that was not the case with the Kimyals.

Siud had presided at the welcome-back feast. I found a chance to ask him, "My legs are bad for sure, but what is the source-thought of naming me Bad Legs?"

"Your bad legs are a big thing to us. In our villages, people with bad legs can't get out of this valley. But even with your bad legs, God brought you all the way here to give us God's Word. People with good legs have come and not stayed. But you, Bad Legs, God has helped you stay with us. He did all this because he loves us."

Bad Legs. What a great name!

A day during my first year at Korupun came to mind. That day I was sitting with some small boys at the end of the airstrip, looking down into the deep river gorge below us. Putting to use the linguistic skills of learning a previously unanalyzed language, I was trying to solve some points of grammar by testing with both use and listening. I talked about my original polio.

"The doctors told my parents, 'Somagdoblag'" (She might die).

"Somagdobso," one of the boys corrected me.

"Y-yes," I said, not sure what that meant. Switching from conversationalist to analyst, after some probing, I discovered that the boys were right—Somagdobso meant "She will likely die." Many children with symptoms as severe as mine did die.

"But you didn't," the boys continued, "because God wanted you to come here and give us his Word."

What simple insight. Far greater insight than that of all those people who told me while I was growing up and training that becoming a missionary was an impossible goal for someone like me. They didn't understand. Siud and those boys did understand. My bad legs weren't a hindrance. They were a tool—God's tool to show the Kimyals how very, very much he loved them.

Chapter 55

UNHAPPY LEGS, ANGRY TICKER

About a year into my fourth term, in 1990, I began to feel unhappy changes in my body. Walking up to Jessie's house made my leg muscles and knees feel sore and weak. Was I worn down from diseases, or was it something else?

At the same time, but having nothing to do with my leg pain, I sensed that maybe God was asking me to prepare for new spheres of work. In my mind, I was at Korupun for another twenty years, but the needs of the tribe—except translation—were changing. God would sort it all out.

My physical heart began "talking" to me more often too. *What is going on?*

During my high school years, sometimes when I yelled too vigorously during basketball games, my heart would do a couple of quick hard beats and felt like there was cotton in it. Then everything returned to normal. No big deal, or so I thought.

I had mentally dismissed those moments so thoroughly that I didn't even remember them until the first time my heart went into faster beats for one to twelve hours at a time during my second and third furloughs back in the United States. By lying on my stomach with my ribs on the edge of my bed, I discovered the resulting pressure of my ribs on my heart got my racing heart back into a normal rhythm. I told no one about it though. If known, would RBMU order me away from Irian Jaya? Maybe. I wasn't going to risk it.

But in August 1990, at Korupun, I had an episode that I could not stop. Our nurse, Jessie, was away on vacation, so I couldn't ask her to help. Orin and Rosa Kidd were in the US. The Kimyals wouldn't know what to do to help me. The weather was not safe for flying, so I couldn't ask for an emergency plane. But I had to ask a doctor for help.

I waited for Dr. Ken Dresser's regularly scheduled late afternoon time to open his communication radio for medical calls. I hoped that few others around the island listened in as I told him, "Ken, my heart has been beating hard and fast for about fourteen hours, and I can't get it under control."

"How fast?"

"It's not easy to count, but it seems to be 180 to 200 beats a minute."

"What have you done to get it back to normal?"

I told him that I tried everything that had worked in the past, but this time they failed. Dr. Ken had no other suggestions. "I will leave my radio on. Call me again when you get the fast beat stopped," he said.

Each beat was so violent that I could see my chest jump with each one. At eighteen hours, I knew I was in danger; I was getting weak, and my body seemed to want to give up.

I prayed one of those Peter-sinking-into-the-water "Lord, help!" kind of prayers. I simply said, "I'm running out of time. Neither Dr. Ken's suggestions nor my usual methods have worked. I'm going to lie down and try again. Please put into my mind what to do."

I did what I said, and God did what I asked. I filled my lungs, held my breath, and used my chest muscles to press my heart against my ribs as hard as I could until I couldn't help but let my breath out. Then my heart stopped racing. Stopped, period. I waited, listening, wondering if it would start again. As if reluctant, it beat one superstrong long beat, then laboriously lumbered along for a minute or two until it settled into a normal rhythm. And I began to hurt. Bad.

I got up, called Ken, and reported that all was well. But it wasn't. My chest was in tremendous pain, and I was so exhausted I could hardly move. I didn't want to say that on the radio, though, lest ears other than Ken's hear it. *I'll write him a letter,* I decided, not knowing when I would have a chance to send one out.

The pain was intense. I knew my heart and chest muscles were bruised, and my heart was exhausted. In the morning, I consciously willed each leg to take the steps to my kitchen where I made a quiche from local eggs and a box of biscuit mix someone had sent me in a package from Chattaroy. That was the simplest thing I could think of to make, and it would last a few days. It was Saturday, so Yaso wouldn't be there to cook for me. I knew I had to eat to give my body strength, but I also knew I did not have in me the ability to prepare more than one thing. I lived on that one quiche and powdered milk for three days while I lay in my small recliner and cried.

I cried because of the pain, because of the weakness, because of relief that I was alive, because of unknown reasons, and because of fear. *What did this mean? What was happening to my body?* It wasn't just my heart—my central nervous system felt like it was falling apart.

Kimyal friends often dropped in to visit or check up on me. When I said I was not well, their response was a shrugged shoulder or a soft chuckle as if I'd told a joke. Finally, Sa'ale said, "Sick! You don't look sick! At least when we are sick, we look like it. Our hair looks sick, our face looks sick, our skin looks sick—you don't look sick!"

He was right. The Kimyals, always drama masters, make sure they look sick when they are. They smear their hair, faces, and chests with pig grease and black ashes and, if they have one, put a dirty rag or torn net bag over their heads. Then they walk with a slouch and put on a long, long face. Everyone knows they are sick. No doubt about it.

I sent a letter to Doctor Ken on the next plane that came to Korupun. I described in detail the racing-heart incident and the pain-filled, exhausted aftermath. My memo reached Dr. Dresser quickly, and he arranged flights for me to meet him at Wamena. He wanted to record a paper strip on his portable EKG unit, then take it with him to Toronto, Canada, where he would be for several months' furlough. He would show the EKG results to a cardiologist friend in Toronto. "I will send a message with the results," he said.

That message told me the type of tachycardia I had, prescribed medication, and mentioned, "Perhaps it is a part of post-polio sequelae in this case."

That was not what I wanted to hear. I had recently heard about this phenomenon, post-polio syndrome, on short-wave radio, Voice of America. *Could it be true? Am I faced with post-polio syndrome? If so, what will that mean?*

Chapter 56

WHAT TO DO?

Early in 1991, my questions and fears took form in a letter to friends:

> Now what are these knee problems? It would be nice
> to say I've worn them out praying, but I'm afraid that
> isn't the case. For at least a year I have noticed intense,
> frequent pain in my knees when I am on them too
> long. A few weeks ago, that could be as short as twenty
> minutes, but now sometimes only five or ten minutes.
> In the last three months, they have gone into a different
> stage, with a different kind of pain. They need less and
> sometimes no provocation. My mobility is drastically
> decreased. Sometimes I can't even hobble into the next
> room without supporting myself on someone or a chair
> back or something. It was never quite that bad before.
> I've arranged for some crutches to come in this week,
> so we'll see if that helps.

> The first thing that comes to my mind when I wonder
> what is happening is post-polio syndrome. I don't know
> much about it though, except that it is affecting people
> around my age who got polio during or before the
> time I did. Whether it is post-polio syndrome or not,
> something has sure been going on. Jessie has an idea
> that sounds like a logical possibility too: that maybe the
> cartilage in my knees has worn down, and some nerves
> are pinched.

Dr. Dresser was in Canada, but Dr. Marge Bromley was back
from Australia. Maybe she knew what was happening. I wrote a letter
to Dr. Marge. I explained my symptoms and their progression. I said,

"It feels like my whole central nervous system is exploding. Could it be post-polio syndrome?" Then, by radio, I asked her to expect my letter.

Two weeks later, Dr. Marge stood at the top of her mountain airstrip watching an airplane take off. She opened the mailbag it had brought and found my letter. She read it and thought, "I don't know what post-polio syndrome is. Lord, how am I going to help Elinor?" At that moment, she looked up and saw someone coming up the airstrip. A trekker with a walking stick—unmistakably a rare Western tourist. He probably wanted her help to ask the local people for food and a place to sleep, so she waited.

When the tourist reached the top of the strip, Dr. Marge introduced herself, and he did too. He was an American doctor, a neurologist. Perfect. Dr. Marge read my letter to him. "Can you give me some advice? Is it post-polio?" she asked.

"It sounds like it could be post-polio syndrome, but we can't know for sure without tests," the doctor said. "She needs to go to the States and be examined."

I didn't like that answer, but I could not dispute God's timing in sending this neurologist along.

In another letter home, I wrote:

> There are some who think I should go home right away
> and get checked out, and on bad days I wonder, too,
> if I will be able to hold out until mid-1992 furlough.
> I don't want to go before then if I can at all avoid it. If
> Dr. Marge Bromley finally recommends that, I'll agree,
> after maybe a bit of negotiation of how soon. (smile)
> I'm hoping the pain will level out soon. On good days,
> I quickly forget and wonder what the fuss is all about.
> My knees aren't going to be any better in America than
> they are here. I don't think much can be done for them.
> I trust the field leadership and Doctor Marge to monitor
> things and do what is right by both my knees and me.

My mind went back to a dream Siud told me about a few weeks earlier. He said, "I saw you leaving Korupun, saying goodbye."

Chapter 57

I LEAVE KORUPUN

Over the next weeks, I pondered Siud's dream and the neurologist's warnings. *Knees can be fixed these days,* I assured myself. *I'll go to Spokane, get them fixed, do the healing and rehab, and be back. This problem doesn't need to mean I can't come back.*

Leaving for good was unthinkable. I still had a lot to do, and Korupun was home. Solidly home. How could I leave these people and this place that had led me to know God as nothing else could have done?

One Sunday morning, I sat on my camp stool on the women's side of the church at Korupun. With only the narrowest path between men and women, people sat skin-to-skin. The scent of grass skirts dominated in the women's section. Toddlers wandered from lap to lap "floating" randomly through the crowd. Babies slept in their net bags or nursed. Sometimes a mom carefully stepped through the other women to carry her baby and net bag outside for a change of the leaves in the bottom of the bag.

Everyone heartily sang Kimyal style or Yali style chant songs, with an Indonesian chorus randomly added. Half a dozen young girls gathered at the front to sing a Melanesian-style song for everyone. People were prayed for. One or two told of something God had done for them that week. No one was in a hurry.

Finally, Siud began his sermon. It was both profound and simple, built around basic Bible passages about Jesus and how following Jesus changes lives. At the end, he stood with tears streaming down his face and said, "We used to walk in the darkness, and now we walk in the Light."

I can still see that so vividly that if I were an artist, I could paint it. Inwardly I said, *Lord, if I had to leave Korupun now, I would be satisfied. Seeing and hearing this is enough.*

———— ⚬⚬⚬ ————

That church service took place not long before the scene that opened this book, when I sat on a riverside rock, visited with friends, and contemplated what my body was doing.

I did have to leave that home. Less than a year later, I boarded an airplane in Sentani on the north coast, where I had first landed in Papua almost eighteen years before. The timing was right so that a son of missionary friends could travel with me on his way to Canada for college. I could no longer walk through airports. I needed help with luggage and help to get wheelchair assistance.

Among the friends who sat with me in the tiny Sentani airport before my flight was Otto, one of the Yali men I met all those years earlier, after the earthquake, as I waited at Ninia to return to Korupun. He was one of the men who had made sure I would not be trampled if an earthquake hit while we were in church. Otto and his wife now lived at Sentani where he had electricity to run the computer John Wilson gave him to work on translating the Old Testament from Indonesian into Yali.

A few days before, Otto and his wife had come to my guest-house for a visit. I could see the care in their eyes. Now here he was with a few others to see me off. When the boarding announcement came, Otto got up, walked with me to the bottom of the steps up to the door of the plane, picked me up, and carried me to the top. Once inside, I cried at that show of love and respect from this man. One who had stepped out of darkness into the light brought by the gospel.

Chapter 58

GOODBYE TO MY KIMYAL FRIENDS

I left Papua thinking I would get my knees fixed and be back in six months or fewer. But then I learned that it wasn't my knees, it was my whole body. I could no longer live there. Not knowing that fact, I had neither packed my things nor said goodbye to my Kimyal friends.

Roger and Gail Smith, friends in the US, heard that and offered to take me back to Korupun to get a few things and say goodbye. They would do that at their expense. What a special gift. My friend Sue Trenier left her work at Soba to help me sort through things and to help the Smiths communicate with the Kimyals who knew some Indonesian.

While we were at Korupun, I scheduled a time in my office to talk to the church leaders. I was very weak. I couldn't sit up, so the Smiths and Sue put a cot in my office so I could lie down and talk to the Kimyal church leaders. They were very shocked to see me like that and upset to know that I wouldn't be with them anymore. They asked, "What is God doing? Why is God letting this happen to you? We thought God's work for you was to give us his Word. Were we wrong? Was that not God's work for you?"

I silently prayed, "Lord, help me. Give me a way to explain this to them."

I remembered the Kimyal people's love of word pictures. They use images and metaphors all the time. I love that way of talking too. From my cot, I looked at the lightbulb in the ceiling. These men had watched and even helped Mike Johnson put in the hydro-electric system. They had helped string the lines and put in the bulbs in rooms.

I said, "That light bulb up there—if that light wasn't on, could we see each other? Could we see anything in this room? When the light is on, it makes clear what is in this room. If that light wasn't there, we couldn't see all the things. That's kind of like the truth about God. If it's not shining, people can't see him rightly.

"But does that lightbulb need arms and legs to shine? What is its job? Its job is just to shine. How does it shine? Not with arms and legs. The only way it can shine is by accepting the power that flows through it.

"If the wire was cut, and that power wasn't going through it, the bulb couldn't shine. It doesn't have any power to shine on its own. That's like you and me. Our real job—my real job—is to shine God's glory. I don't need strong arms and legs to do that. All I need to do is accept the power of God and let it flow through my life. That's my real job. Where and how I do it—that's up to him. Whether it's here at Korupun, doing that here with you, translating the Scriptures for you, or whether it's back in America.

"In the Bible, the apostle Paul said that when he complained to God about his weakness, God said, 'My grace is all you need because my power shows up best in your weakness.' Paul understood and said, 'When I am weak, then I am strong.'

"In my weakness, God's strong power can show up."

I live in America now, but here, Chattaroy, must forever share with Korupun the spot in my heart called "home." Korupun is in my bones and in my soul. It is where God showed me that he is enough. More than enough.

EPILOGUE

Whenever people hear parts of this story or see the video version, "Bad Legs,"[1] they want to know, "What do you do now?"

A year after I left Papua, I had to retire. My body could no longer sustain even a quarter-time regular job.

Now I write various kinds of items, and I put together the children's publication, "Great Commission Kids." My favorite thing is regularly mentoring future and current missionaries. I keep frequent contact with young Kimyal people through social media. I love to speak as my body lets me. And I give my dog Marco a long walk or two every day, using my outdoor mobility scooter. That is a great time to think and pray.

In a way, those years in Papua were preparation for what I do now. They give credibility, a wide reach, and a solid impact to the mentoring, writing, speaking, and encouraging that I do.

Expect more stories.[2]

---

1 https://www.youtube.com/watch?v=5ooDQsHvUmw&t=15s
2 elinoryoung.com

ACKNOWLEDGMENTS

Writing this book took way longer and was way harder than I thought it would be. A whole flock of people helped me. Just a thank-you doesn't say enough, and I cannot cover everybody without consuming pages to do it. So here goes a condensed version.

To my fellow writers and the staff at my first Oregon Christian Writers Summer Conference—I was blown away by the warmth with which I and the other neophytes were received. Far from exuding a "we have arrived" attitude, your approach was "we're in this together." You took great joy in encouraging and helping us newbies. You did that for me then and have continued to do so. Thank you!

To my writer friend Gwen, who comforted and encouraged me when, at an earlier conference by another organization, a snooty presenter sarcastically snapped at me, "Just write for your polio friends." You, Gwen, comforted me in my tears, helped me regain my footing, and keep going. Some weeks later you gently suggested tips and an outline idea for the whole story. It was what guided me throughout. Thank you, sweet friend!

To my beta readers, who also copy- and story-line edited along the way: Taylor, Kari, and Sylvia—you helped make something that was OK into something that began to look pretty good. Sharman and Betty Sue—your job was to write endorsements, but in the process, you became virtual beta readers-cum-copyeditors too. Thanks so much, all of you!

To Rachel Lulich, my developmental editor (who sometimes couldn't help but copyedit too)—you showed me where to add detail that was missing, cut out distracting detail, order things more logically, and in the process, taught me those writerly things called arc and flow. Thank you, Rachel. I'm so glad you took on my project. You didn't have the time, but you did it.

I can't draw. Period. But I have artistic friends who freely offered their talents to this book project. Thank you, Wren Johannson, for the gorgeous front cover design, and thank you, Anne Stoothoff, for the equally beautiful map of Papua. Wow.

And a big thank-you to uncountable local and international friends who have spurred me on and even prayed about this multi-year project.

My Kimyal friends—some of you can read English, but to all of you I want to say, "A'un nisin wana' ulamsin. A'undi gibna' yubu di babe, na se doa yubu di babe sob-sob arolamnelom. Anda, na'abo aboga gibsin."

BEAUTIFUL FEET UPON THE MOUNTAINS

Bible Visuals International offers a full-page illustrated and teachable children's version of the story in this book. You may order *Beautiful Feet upon the Mountains* in various formats. Go to Biblevisuals.org and click on "Materials," then "Stories." Contact them at Biblevisuals.org/contact/.

ORDER INFORMATION

To order additional copies of this book, please visit
www.redemption-press.com.
Also available on Amazon.com and BarnesandNoble.com
or by calling toll-free 1-844-2REDEEM.